The Importance Of

James Baldwin

These and other titles are included in The Importance
Of biography series:

THE IMPORTANCE OF

James Baldwin

by
James Tackach

Lucent Books, P.O. Box 289011, San Diego, CA 92198-9011

Library of Congress Cataloging-in-Publication Data

Tackach, James
    James Baldwin / James Tackach.
      p. cm.—(The Importance of)
    Includes bibliographical references (p.   ) and index.
    Summary: Discusses the life of James Baldwin, his activism
in civil rights, and the importance of his writings.
    ISBN 1-56006-070-0 (alk. paper)
    1. Baldwin, James, 1924–1987—Biography—Juvenile
literature.   2. Afro-American authors—20th century—
Biography—Juvenile literature.   3. Civil rights workers—
United States—Biography—Juvenile literature.   [1. Baldwin,
James, 1924–1987.   2. Authors, American.   3. Civil rights
workers.   4. Gay men—Biography.   5. Afro-Americans—
Biography.]   I. Title.   II. Series.
   PS3552.A45Z915   1997
   818'.5409—dc20   96–14185
   [B]   CIP
                                            AC

Copyright 1997 by Lucent Books, Inc., P.O. Box 289011,
San Diego, California, 92198-9011

Printed in the U.S.A.

Contents

Foreword

THE IMPORTANCE OF biography series deals with individuals who have made a unique contribution to history. The editors of the series have deliberately chosen to cast a wide net and include people from all fields of endeavor. Individuals from politics, music, art, literature, philosophy, science, sports, and religion are all represented. In addition, the editors did not restrict the series to individuals whose accomplishments have helped change the course of history. Of necessity, this criterion would have eliminated many whose contribution was great, though limited. Charles Darwin, for example, was responsible for radically altering the scientific view of the natural history of the world. His achievements continue to impact the study of science today. Others, such as Chief Joseph of the Nez Percé, played a pivotal role in the history of their own people. While Joseph's influence does not extend much beyond the Nez Percé, his nonviolent resistance to white expansion and his continuing role in protecting his tribe and his homeland remain an inspiration to all.

These biographies are more than factual chronicles. Each volume attempts to emphasize an individual's contributions both in his or her own time and for posterity. For example, the voyages of Christopher Columbus opened the way to European colonization of the New World. Unquestionably, his encounter with the New World brought monumental changes to both Europe and the Americas in his day. Today, however, the broader impact of Columbus's voyages is being critically scrutinized. *Christopher Columbus,* as well as every biography in The Importance Of series, includes and evaluates the most recent scholarship available on each subject.

Each author includes a wide variety of primary and secondary source quotations to document and substantiate his or her work. All quotes are footnoted to show readers exactly how and where biographers derive their information, as well as provide stepping stones to further research. These quotations enliven the text by giving readers eyewitness views of the life and times of each individual covered in The Importance Of series.

Finally, each volume is enhanced by photographs, bibliographies, chronologies, and comprehensive indexes. For both the casual reader and the student engaged in research, The Importance Of biographies will be a fascinating adventure into the lives of people who have helped shape humanity's past and present, and who will continue to shape its future.

IMPORTANT DATES IN THE LIFE OF
JAMES BALDWIN

1924
Baldwin is born in Harlem.

1936–1938
Attends Frederick Douglass Junior High School.

1938–1942
Attends DeWitt Clinton High School.

1942–1943
Works in New Jersey for the U.S. Army.

1943
David Baldwin, James's stepfather, dies.

1945
Wins Eugene F. Saxton Trust grant.

1947
Reviews Maxim Gorky short story collection for the *Nation*.

1948
Publishes first essay, "The Harlem Ghetto," and first short story, "Previous Condition." Departs for Paris.

1953
Publishes first novel, *Go Tell It on the Mountain*.

1955
Publishes *Notes of a Native Son*. First play, *The Amen Corner*, is performed at Howard University.

1956
Publishes *Giovanni's Room*.

1957
Returns to the United States and tours the South.

1961
Publishes *Nobody Knows My Name*.

1962
Publishes *Another Country*.

1963
Publishes *The Fire Next Time*. Participates in the March on Washington for jobs and freedom.

1964
Blues for Mister Charlie opens on Broadway.

1965
Publishes *Going to Meet the Man*, a short story collection.

1968
Martin Luther King Jr. is murdered in Memphis. Baldwin publishes *Tell Me How Long the Train's Been Gone*.

1971
Publishes *A Rap on Race* with Margaret Mead.

1972
Publishes *No Name in the Street* and *One Day, When I Was Lost*.

1974
Publishes *If Beale Street Could Talk*.

1976
Publishes *The Devil Finds Work*.

1978–1981
Teaches at Bowling Green University.

1979
Publishes *Just Above My Head*.

1983–1986
Teaches at five colleges in Amherst, Massachusetts.

1985
Publishes *The Evidence of Things Not Seen* and *The Price of the Ticket*.

1987
Dies in Saint Paul-de-Vence, France.

A Writer and Activist

The American Civil Rights movement of the 1950s and 1960s produced many heroes. With his eloquent speeches and charismatic leadership, the Reverend Martin Luther King Jr. awakened America to its racial inequities and prompted black Americans to fight for their constitutional rights and liberties. With his elegant and energetic play on the baseball diamond, Jackie Robinson opened the field of sports to African Americans. An ordinary Alabama woman named Rosa Parks refused to give up her bus seat to a white man and triggered a movement that abolished segregation in the American South. Thurgood Marshall fought injustice in America's courtrooms and became the first African American to serve on the U.S. Supreme Court.

The name James Baldwin can be added to this impressive list. Baldwin's weapons in the civil rights struggle were

In 1955, Rosa Parks (pictured) made history when she was arrested for refusing to give up her bus seat to a white man. Her arrest sparked a movement that ended segregation in the South.

his pen and his typewriter. In his many novels, essays, and plays, Baldwin examined the racial and civil rights issues that most Americans had never confronted. Early in his career, Baldwin explained the special function that a writer plays in American society: "to describe things which other people are too busy to describe"—more specifically, to strip away "a myth about America to which we are clinging which has nothing to do with the lives we lead."[1] The myth to which Baldwin referred was the widespread belief that America's constitutional guarantees of freedom and equality applied to all American citizens.

The Fourteenth and Fifteenth Amendments to the U.S. Constitution, passed shortly after the Civil War, theoretically guaranteed citizenship and voting rights to all Americans. Nonetheless, a century would pass before most African Americans began to enjoy these constitutional guarantees. In the South, black Americans faced the insults and indignities of lawful segregation. They were restricted to certain seating areas in restaurants, theaters, and sports arenas, and they could not vote or run for public office. In the North racial prejudice was, perhaps, less overt, yet African Americans were prohibited from living in certain neighborhoods,

A young black man drinks from a water fountain clearly marked with the word "colored," meaning for blacks only. Through his writing, James Baldwin worked to expose and combat the indignities of segregation.

James Baldwin's work as writer, public speaker, social critic, and racial activist helped push the country to confront racial injustice.

attending some schools, and entering many professions.

Changes began to occur, however, after World War II. In 1947 Jackie Robinson integrated major league baseball. That same year the Supreme Court outlawed discrimination in America's law schools. A year later President Harry Truman ended the practice of segregated battalions for white and black servicemen. For perhaps the first time, many Americans began to realize that their country's citizens of color were denied political, social, and economic opportunities and that this situation needed to be remedied.

During the 1950s and 1960s, a great many civil rights battles were fought and won. School segregation was outlawed, as was segregation in restaurants, hotels, theaters, and other public places. Voting rights were extended to those citizens who had previously been turned away at the ballot box. Employment and housing restrictions were gradually eased.

James Baldwin played an important role during these two crucial decades. Foremost as a writer, but also as a public speaker, social critic, and racial activist, Baldwin helped prompt a complacent country to confront racial injustice. Racism has not, unfortunately, been eradicated in the United States, despite the contributions of Baldwin and others. Nonetheless, because of Americans like James Baldwin, the United States is a more just and less segregated nation.

1 A Harlem Boyhood

James Baldwin never knew his father. His mother, Emma Berdis Jones, was unmarried when she gave birth to James in Harlem Hospital on August 2, 1924; and she never revealed his father's name to her son, though James often asked her for it. In 1927 Emma Jones married David Baldwin, a factory worker and part-time preacher, and the family took his name.

During the next fifteen years, David and Emma Baldwin had eight children. The United States was suffering through the Great Depression during these years, and keeping the Baldwin family clothed and fed was a terrible struggle. In one of his essays, Baldwin described his childhood as "the usual bleak fantasy" that he "certainly would not consider living . . . again."[2]

The family lived in the section of Harlem bordered by Lenox Avenue on the west, the Harlem River on the east, 135th Street on the north, and 130th Street on the south—an area Baldwin later called his "turf."[3] The Baldwins could never afford to buy their own home, and they rented a succession of tenement apartments that Baldwin later described as "cheerless as a prison."[4]

David Baldwin was a southerner, the son of ex-slaves, born and raised in Louisiana after the Civil War, when freed slaves faced the harshest forms of discrimi-

nation. He left New Orleans in 1919; like thousands of other African Americans at that time, he moved north, hoping to find justice and economic opportunity. He had married, fathered children, and become widowed before meeting and marrying Emma Jones. He was almost forty years her senior and brought to her household his son and elderly mother. While still living in the South, he had been a traveling minister, preaching the gospel to the former slaves who lived in rural Louisiana, and he continued preaching in Harlem's storefront churches after moving north.

A Strict Upbringing

Mr. Baldwin was an angry man, his personality shaped by his bitter experiences. While living in the South, he had heard of black men lynched without trial. He had seen black workers beaten by their employers for trivial reasons. In the North, the discrimination was less harsh, but most black people lived in squalid conditions, crowded in urban slums where poverty, filth, drugs, and crime made life miserable.

Mr. Baldwin hated and mistrusted most white people. He constantly warned

A neighborhood street in Harlem, much like the one where James Baldwin spent his childhood years. The Baldwins were unable to afford their own home and rented a succession of dreary tenement apartments.

his children that whites could not be their friends because, as James later recalled,

> White people would do anything to keep a Negro down. Some of them could be nice, he admitted, but none of them were to be trusted and most of them were not even nice. The best thing was to have as little to do with them as possible.[5]

Mr. Baldwin was also suspicious of people who were not Christian. Once when James was in high school, he brought home a white friend. When the visitor left,

Mr. Baldwin asked James if his friend was a Christian. James answered that his friend was Jewish, and Mr. Baldwin's powerful hand came down across his stepson's face. Mr. Baldwin did not approve of James associating with white, non-Christian companions.

Mr. Baldwin ruled his family very strictly. Believing that the streets of Harlem were the territory of Satan, Mr. Baldwin tried to keep his children safely in their apartment as much as possible. They would look out the window in envy as the neighborhood youngsters played

Baldwin's stepfather believed the streets of Harlem were the territory of Satan, so he kept his children confined to their apartment. Baldwin and his siblings had to be content with watching from the window as the rest of the neighborhood children played outside.

stickball or hopscotch in the street. When James or one of his siblings failed to heed any of their father's edicts, the disobedient child was usually subjected to a beating and a stern punishment.

Baldwin often said that he hated his stepfather and at times wished to kill him. Wisely, he turned to his mother and stepgrandmother for solace when his stepfather became too abusive. His stepgrandmother, Barbara Baldwin, lived with the family in Harlem for a time, and she would scold her son when he was too harsh with his children. James would often find sanctuary in her room, where she would entertain him with tales of the South be-

fore the Civil War. The elderly woman instilled in the boy a respect for his slave ancestors and his heritage. Baldwin later wrote that when his stepgrandmother died, his heart was broken—"because I had loved her and depended on her. I knew—children *must* know—that she would always protect me with all her strength."[6]

James's mother also protected her children against their father's angry moods. But James later wrote that his mother

paid an immense price for standing between us and our father. He had ways of making her suffer quite beyond our ken, and so we soon learned to depend on each other and became a kind of wordless conspiracy to protect *her*.[7]

Hence, James formed very close bonds with his eight siblings and stayed close to them throughout his life. He later credited his siblings with saving him from a terrible fate: "They kept me so busy caring for them, keeping them from the rats, roaches, falling plaster, and all the banality of poverty that I had no time to become a junkie or an alcoholic."[8]

School Days

Like most other city youngsters, James Baldwin attended the local public schools. He was a somewhat shy, unathletic boy, and he did not make friends easily. His stepfather had nicknamed him "frog eyes" because of his large eyes; hence, James was convinced that he was ugly and that his classmates would not want to befriend him.

But James's teachers quickly recognized his talent and intelligence and encouraged him. Orilla Miller, a teacher at P. S. 24, James's grade school, sensed that the boy had an interest in literature and language, and she took him to see Shakespearean plays performed on Broadway at her own expense. Miss Miller was white, and therefore mistrusted by Mr. Baldwin, but she served as a mentor for James for several years and even supplied the family with groceries when Mr. Baldwin lost his job.

After graduating from P.S. 24, James attended P.S. 139, also known as Frederick Douglass Junior High School. Countee Cullen, the great African American poet,

taught French at the school, and James made his acquaintance. By this time James had developed a keen interest in books. He claimed to have read every book at the local Harlem library; so after school and on Saturdays, he would venture downtown to the main branch of the New York Public Library on 42nd Street. On one such journey, James was exposed to the kind of blatant racism that he had not yet confronted in Harlem. As James crossed Fifth

While attending Frederick Douglass Junior High School, James Baldwin made the acquaintance of Countee Cullen (pictured), the great African American poet, who taught French at the school.

Baldwin recalls the Harlem streets where he spent his childhood as being dirty and crowded. Buildings were old and falling apart, and the cost of living was far beyond the means of many residents.

Avenue on his way to the library, a white policeman asked him, "Why don't you niggers stay uptown where you belong?"[9] Baldwin later referred to this unpleasant incident as an example of the "incessant and gratuitous humiliation and danger" that black citizens "encountered every working day, all day long."[10]

But James continued his quest for books. He was constantly reading, sometimes holding a younger brother or sister in one arm and grasping Harriet Beecher Stowe's *Uncle Tom's Cabin* or Charles Dickens's *A Tale of Two Cities* with his free hand. James's appetite for books spurred an interest in writing. He excelled on the writ-

ten reports that his teachers required; one of his junior high school teachers claimed that James was a better writer than most of the other teachers and the school principal. He frequently contributed articles and stories to his school literary magazine, the *Douglass Pilot;* and in his final year at Frederick Douglass Junior High, James was named the magazine's editor.

A Religious Conversion

It was just after he completed junior high school, in the summer of 1938, that James had a religious experience that would profoundly affect him for many years. The Baldwin family had always been deeply religious. Mr. Baldwin, who served as a deacon at the Abyssinian Baptist Church on 138th Street, demanded that his family attend church services every Saturday evening and Sunday morning.

Moreover, in church and at home young James heard a never-ending sermon on the necessity of avoiding sin and on the retribution that an angry God would soon bestow upon his people. The environment in which James was raised seemed to confirm these warnings. He later wrote that "the wages of sin were visible everywhere, in every wine-stained and urine-splashed hallway, in every clanging ambulance bell."[11] And Harlem was filled with wasted lives. Baldwin described seeing boys his own age "in twos and threes and fours, in a hallway, sharing a jug of wine or a bottle of whiskey, talking, cursing, fighting, sometimes weeping: lost, and unable to say what it was that oppressed them."[12]

Raised on Books

James Baldwin opens Notes of a Native Son, *his first collection of essays (published in 1955), with a brief autobiographical sketch. Its opening paragraph shows his early interest in reading and writing.*

"I was born in Harlem, thirty-one years ago. I began plotting novels at about the time I learned to read. The story of my childhood is the usual bleak fantasy, and we can dismiss it with the restrained observation that I certainly would not consider living it again. In those days my mother was given to the exasperating and mysterious habit of having babies. As they were born, I took them over with one hand and held a book with the other. The children probably suffered, though they have since been kind enough to deny it, and in this way I read *Uncle Tom's Cabin* and *A Tale of Two Cities* over and over and over again; in this way, in fact, I read just about everything I could get my hands on—except the Bible, probably because it was the only book I was encouraged to read. I must also confess that I wrote—a great deal—and my first professional triumph, in any case, the first effort of mine to be seen in print, occurred at the age of twelve or thereabouts, when a short story I had written about the Spanish revolution won some prize in an extremely short-lived church newspaper. I remember the story was censored by the lady editor, though I don't remember why, and I was outraged."

Even as a fourteen-year-old boy, James sensed that he would have to take some extreme measures to avoid this disastrous fate. Years later, he explained his reaction this way:

Just before and then during the Second World War, many of my friends fled into the service, all to be changed there, and rarely for the better, many to be ruined, and many to die. Others fled to other states and cities—that is, to other ghettos. Some went on wine or whiskey or the needle, and are still on it. And others, like me, fled to the church. [13]

James began to attend the nearby Mount Calvary of the Pentecostal Faith Church with his best friend; he was impressed by its dynamic minister, known to her congregation as Mother Horn, one of Harlem's few female preachers. Late in the summer of 1938, during one of Mother Horn's moving sermons, James experienced a dramatic religious revelation. He rose from his seat, approached the altar, and fell to the floor. He felt, as he later put it, an anguish that "moved . . . like one of those floods that devastate counties, tearing everything down, tearing children from their parents and lovers

The Harlem Ghetto

In an essay titled "The Harlem Ghetto," originally published in Commentary *magazine in 1948 and included in the collection* Notes of a Native Son, *James Baldwin gives a vivid description of the Harlem ghetto that he knew as a child.*

"Harlem, physically at least, has changed very little in my parents' lifetime or in mine. Now as then the buildings are old and in desperate need of repair, the streets are crowded and dirty, there are too many human beings per square block. Rents are 10 to 58 per cent higher than anywhere else in the city; food, expensive everywhere, is more expensive here and of an inferior quality; and now that the war is over and money is dwindling, clothes are carefully shopped for and seldom bought. Negroes, traditionally the last to be hired and the first to be fired, are finding jobs harder and harder to get, and, while prices are rising implacably, wages are going down. All over Harlem now there is felt the bitter expectancy with which, in my childhood, we awaited winter: it is coming and it will be hard; there is nothing anyone can do about it.

All of Harlem is pervaded by a sense of congestion, rather like the insistent, maddening, claustrophobic pounding in the skull that comes from trying to breathe in a very small room with all the windows shut."

from each other, and making everything an unrecognizable waste."[14]

The Fire and Excitement of the Church

James interpreted the experience as a sign from God that he was destined to be saved from the wreckage around him. He immediately became determined to save others as well. Under Mother Horn's tutelage he began to train for the ministry. In a very short time, James was named a junior minister, which meant that he was permitted to deliver sermons in neighborhood churches.

James was quickly in great demand. He overcame his shyness and became a dynamic public speaker. With just a few notes in front of him, he delivered powerful sermons that greatly moved worshipers. They fell to their knees or threw up their arms screaming for God's forgiveness. Years later Baldwin still had vivid memories of his most moving sermons:

> The church was very exciting. . . .
> There is no music like that music, no drama like the drama of the saints rejoicing, the sinners moaning, the tambourines racing, and all those voices coming together and crying holy unto the Lord. . . . I have never seen anything to equal the fire and excitement that sometimes, without warning, fill a church, causing the church . . . to "rock." Nothing that has happened to me since equals the power and the glory that I sometimes felt when, in the middle of a sermon, I knew that I was somehow, by some miracle, really

carrying, as they said, "the Word"—when the church and I were one.[15]

James preached for three years, and the entire Baldwin family predicted that he would become a great minister with a grand following, but James's life took another turn.

In the fall of 1938, James began attending DeWitt Clinton High School in the Bronx. It was a new experience for James in several ways. It took him out of his neighborhood every day. He had always attended neighborhood schools, but Harlem had no high school. His new school was integrated, so James was, for the first time in his life, forced to deal with white people on a daily basis.

Seeds of Doubt

More importantly, perhaps, DeWitt Clinton High served the large number of Jewish families who lived in the Bronx during the 1930s; so for the first time, James interacted and formed friendships with young people who were not Christian. When young Minister Baldwin passed out religious literature to his new classmates, they laughed at him. When James used passages from the Bible to defend his views on social or political issues, his friends effectively challenged his arguments, which subtly shook his religious faith. He began to doubt whether strong faith alone could improve the wretched conditions under which most black people lived. He had seen too many Harlem boys from devout religious families—youngsters he had seen praying during Sunday services—lost to the dreary world of alcohol, drugs, and crime.

Escaping the Slums

In an essay titled "Fifth Avenue, Uptown: A Letter from Harlem," originally published in Esquire *magazine in 1960 and included in the collection* Nobody Knows My Name, *Baldwin comments on the difficulty of escaping the slums.*

"The people . . . are always pointing out that So-and-So, white, and So-and-So, black, rose from the slums into the big time. The existence—the public existence—of, say, Frank Sinatra and Sammy Davis, Jr. proves to them that America is still the land of opportunity and that inequalities vanish before the determined will. It proves nothing of the sort. The determined will is rare—at the moment, in this country, it is unspeakably rare—and the inequalities suffered by the many are in no way justified by the rise of a few."

Baldwin maintained that escaping the bleak slums was difficult and rare.

James continued to devour books, which he later said was mainly responsible for "the slow crumbling of my faith."[16] The novels of Fyodor Dostoyevsky, the great nineteenth-century Russian writer, and Charles Dickens, the author of *Oliver Twist*, *Hard Times*, and other tales of London's slums, replaced his Bible. As an African American, James identified with the politically oppressed protagonists of Dostoyevsky's novels, and he appreciated the way Dickens captured the squalor of urban life in nineteenth-century England.

James continued to deliver searing Sunday sermons, but he also composed short stories and poems for publication in the *Magpie*, his school's literary magazine. Many of his poems and stories dealt with religious issues, but James also displayed the ability to confront the social and political issues of the day through his writing. For example, "Black Girl Shouting," a poem published in the *Magpie*, featured a young girl whose lover had been lynched:

> Black girl, hide
> Your bitterness.
>
> Black girl, stretch
> Your mouth so wide.
> None will guess
> The way he died
>
> Turned your heart
> To quivering Mud
> While your lover's
> Soft, red blood
>
> Stained the scowling
> Outraged tree.[17]

One story, "Peace on Earth," depicts four soldiers who are reading the Bible shortly before a Christmas Day battle. As shells begin to fall, the narrator asks, "Why is there no peace on earth? Christ came to bring peace."[18]

Possibilities

Because of his writing skills, James was named to the magazine's editorial staff. His fellow editors were Richard Avedon and Emile Capouya, both of whom would later become influential New York editors and publishers. During his junior year in high school, Capouya introduced Baldwin to Beauford Delaney, a noted African American painter who lived in Greenwich Village. In his studio the successful painter lectured the student writer on the importance of art and the role of the artist in their troubled world. Discussing these weighty matters while listening to jazz records, the two formed a friendship that lasted many years. And for the first time, perhaps, James realized that it was possible for a person of his race to become a famous artist. As he considered his future, he became less sure that he wanted to become a minister. David Baldwin, sensing that his stepson was wavering, once asked him on the way home from Sunday church services, "You'd rather write than preach, wouldn't you?" James gave a one-word reply: "Yes."[19] Mr. Baldwin said nothing more, and James later recalled the conversation as the only time that he and his stepfather had had a heart-to-heart talk.

James officially left the church in the spring of 1941, when he was sixteen years old. He later claimed that he walked out of church in the middle of a Sunday service and met his friend Capouya on Broadway for a matinee play performance.

Harlem's Housing Projects

In an essay titled "Fifth Avenue, Uptown: A Letter from Harlem," originally published in Esquire *magazine and included in the collection* Nobody Knows My Name, *James Baldwin vividly describes the bleak housing projects in which he grew up.*

"The projects in Harlem are hated. . . . The projects are hideous, of course, there being a law, apparently respected throughout the world, that popular housing shall be as cheerless as a prison. They are lumped all over Harlem, colorless, bleak, high, and revolting. The wide windows look out on Harlem's invincible squalor: the Park Avenue railroad tracks, around which, about forty years ago, the present dark community began; the unrehabilitated houses, bowed down, it would seem, under the great weight of frustration and bitterness they contain; the dark, ominous schoolhouses from which the child may emerge maimed, blinded, hooked, or enraged for life; and the churches, churches, block upon block of churches, niched in the walls like cannon in the walls of a fortress."

His life as a young minister was over, yet his experiences in the church would profoundly affect his life and art forever. In his essays, novels, and plays, James Baldwin would often discuss the religious fervor of his youth; he could never leave it behind.

After James left the church, he found himself more regularly at odds with his devoutly religious stepfather. He knew that it was time to leave his family's home and live on his own.

Perhaps because of the tension and confusion in his life, James had failed a few courses during his senior year at Dewitt Clinton High. His class graduated in 1941, and James stayed on for six more months to complete the requirements for his diploma. The caption beside his yearbook picture noted that his goal was to become a novelist and a playwright. One day he would attain that goal; but first, he had to find a job and leave his stepfather's house.

Chapter

2 Leaving Home

After high school graduation, James Baldwin was determined to leave home and make a go of it on his own. First, however, he needed a job, but his only work experience involved the menial positions that he had held after school and on weekends —dishwasher in Greenwich Village restaurants, floor sweeper, errand boy. Baldwin's high school friend, Emile Capouya, came to his rescue. After graduation Capouya had landed a job with the U.S. Army laying railroad track in Belle Mead, New Jersey. When an opening for a new worker became available, Capouya remembered his high school buddy and recommended Baldwin for the job; Baldwin was hired.

Life in New Jersey

Baldwin's new job paid well—eighty dollars per week—and he was able to leave home and move into an apartment with Capouya and his foreman near their place of employment. The work was difficult. Baldwin was a short, slender young man—about five feet six inches tall and 135 pounds—so laying railroad track was a formidable task, but Baldwin was determined to keep at it so that he could

continue to live on his own, independent of his parents.

Perhaps the most difficult part of Baldwin's new job was learning to cope with his coworkers and the local citizenry. While living in New York, Baldwin had seldom encountered overt racism. Only black people lived in his Harlem neighborhood, and he had gotten along well with white students at DeWitt Clinton High School; he had met few white racists in his lifetime.

Baldwin encountered many white racists during the year that he lived in New Jersey. He later recalled:

> I learned in New Jersey that to be a Negro meant, precisely, that one was never looked at but was simply at the mercy of the reflexes the color of one's skin cause in other people. . . . I had scarcely arrived before I had earned the enmity . . . of all my superiors and nearly all my coworkers.[20]

On the job, Baldwin was assigned the most menial and undesirable tasks, and his fellow laborers insulted him regularly.

In his new neighborhood, Baldwin was treated as a second-class citizen. Certain restaurants would not serve him, and the local bowling alley turned him away. One night, after a waitress told him that her diner did not serve black people, Baldwin picked up a water glass and threw it at the mirror behind the counter. He dashed out of the restaurant and was saved from arrest only because his companion managed to misdirect the policeman who was summoned.

Baldwin barely lasted a year in New Jersey. As he later put it, "My reputation in town naturally enhanced my reputation at work and my working day became one long series of acrobatics designed to keep me out of trouble."[21] His acrobatics did not succeed. He was twice fired and rehired, but the third time that he was fired—for taking too long on his lunch break—he was dismissed for good. He would have to return to Harlem.

The Death of David Baldwin

During the months that Baldwin lived in New Jersey, his stepfather's health began to degenerate. He had become increasingly paranoid—prone to unreasonable and imaginary fears. For example, he once claimed that his wife and children were poisoning his food and refused to eat. As time passed Mr. Baldwin's mental and physical health worsened, and his wife eventually had him committed to Central Islip Hospital, a state facility for people suffering from mental illnesses. Mr. Baldwin had also contracted tuberculosis, a lung disease, and that disease took his life in the summer of 1943. Hours after Mr. Baldwin died, his last child, Paula Maria, was born in Harlem Hospital.

Mr. Baldwin's funeral was on August 2, James's nineteenth birthday. As Baldwin sat through the funeral service, he felt very mixed emotions. He regretted that he never communicated very well with his stepfather and later wrote that his poor relationship with his stepfather was all too common in America, that "the second generation has no time to talk to the first."[22] Baldwin remembered the few times that David Baldwin had shown pride in his stepson and the rare times when he was kind and gentle. But Baldwin also remembered the bitter fights they had, "fights of the worst possible kind,"[23] he would later call them.

But James Baldwin took a valuable lesson from his stepfather's death. Commenting on his stepfather's bitter life and death in his most famous essay, "Notes of a Native Son," Baldwin realized that "bitterness was folly. . . . Hatred, which could destroy so much, never failed to destroy the man who hated and this was an immutable law."[24]

Meeting Mr. Wright

Baldwin had moved back to his family's Harlem apartment while his stepfather was hospitalized with the illness that would eventually kill him. To help support his mother and his younger brothers and sisters, Baldwin took odd jobs—meat packer, elevator operator—that did not pay very well.

At this time in his life, Baldwin felt very unsettled. During the previous year, he had left home and returned and he had landed and lost several jobs. His stepfather's death added to his feelings of confusion; he later wrote that David Baldwin's death had made him "wonder about that life and also, in a new way, to be apprehensive about my own."[25] Through this

Baldwin sought guidance on his first novel from author Richard Wright. Wright willingly advised Baldwin, and though the relationship between the two eventually became strained, Baldwin never forgot Wright's help.

period, however, Baldwin never lost sight of his main goal: to become a writer. While living in New Jersey and when he returned to Harlem, Baldwin worked on a succession of stories and essays; he even wrote fifty pages of a novel.

Unsure about what to do with the literary pieces on which he was working, Baldwin sought the help of an established African American writer, Richard Wright. Baldwin had recently read two of Wright's books, *Uncle Tom's Children*, a collection of stories about southern blacks who struggled with the segregated conditions in that region, and *Native Son*, Wright's masterwork, a searing best-selling novel about a black man who accidentally kills the daughter of a white man for whom he is working. These two powerful books had a profound effect on Baldwin, and late in 1944 he decided to seek out their author for advice on his own writings.

Wright, at the time, was living with his family in an apartment in Brooklyn. Baldwin found the address, perhaps in the phone book, and simply knocked on Wright's door. In an interview many years later, Baldwin recalled the bravado that brought a novice writer to the famous author's doorstep: "I just knocked on his door in Brooklyn! Introduced myself, and of course he'd no idea who I was." [26]

Wright was very gracious and very encouraging to the twenty-year-old writer who appeared at his door. He agreed to read the fifty pages of the novel on which Baldwin was working—tentatively titled *Crying Holy*—and to offer his professional assessment and advice. Wright liked what he read. He suggested that Baldwin apply for a grant from the Eugene F. Saxton Trust—a fund established for developing writers—to finish the novel. Baldwin enthusiastically applied, and he was rewarded with a five-hundred-dollar grant, the first payment that he would earn with his pen.

Baldwin remained in contact with Richard Wright for many years. The two would live near each other in Paris for a time, and they would read and comment on each other's books. Though a rift in their relationship would eventually occur, Baldwin always acknowledged the help that Wright had provided when the young, uncertain writer knocked on his apartment door and asked for help.

First Publications

After receiving the Saxton Trust grant, Baldwin worked hard to turn *Crying Holy* into a publishable novel. When he completed it, he sent it to several publishers, including Harper's, Vanguard, and Doubleday, but none of the editors who reviewed his manuscript recommended it for publication.

Undaunted, Baldwin continued to write. Early in 1947 he met the poet Randall Jarrell, an editor of the *Nation*, a noteworthy weekly magazine, and Jarrell commissioned him to write a review of *Best Short Stories* by Russian writer Maxim Gorky. Shortly thereafter Jarrell asked Baldwin to review a new biography of Frederick Douglass, the former slave who had become a great author and statesman during the Civil War era. Other assignments followed—in the *Nation* and in other important journals and magazines. At age twenty-three, Baldwin was establishing himself as a tough and perceptive book reviewer and critic.

Late in 1947 the editors of *Commentary*, a journal published by the American Jewish Committee, encouraged Baldwin to write an essay about the relationship between blacks and Jews in New York City. Relations between the two ethnic groups had always been strained, and Baldwin, an

Richard Wright's Example

Richard Wright was best known for his 1940 blockbuster novel, Native Son. *This passage from the first chapter demonstrates Wright's ability to depict the conditions of life in the African American ghettos, as Bigger Thomas, the novel's protagonist, kills a rat that has made its way into his family's apartment.*

"The rat leaped. Bigger sprang to one side. The rat stopped under a chair and let out a furious screak. Bigger moved slowly backward toward the door.

'Gimme that skillet, Buddy,' he asked quietly, not taking his eyes from the rat.

Buddy extended his hand. Bigger caught the skillet and lifted it high in the air. The rat scuttled across the floor and stopped again at the box and searched quickly for the hole; then it reared once more and bared long yellow fangs, piping shrilly, belly quivering.

Bigger aimed and let the skillet fly with a heavy grunt. There was a shattering of wood as the box caved in. The woman screamed and hid her face in her hands. Bigger tiptoed forward and peered.

'I got 'im,' he muttered, his clenched teeth bared in a smile. 'By God, I got 'im.'"

"The Harlem Ghetto," an essay that addressed relations between blacks and Jews, brought Baldwin renown as a shrewd analyst of America's racial tensions.

African American from Harlem who had made many Jewish friends in high school and thereafter, seemed the perfect commentator to discuss black-Jewish relations. And as David Leeming, a Baldwin biographer and critic, asserted, "Baldwin approached his subject with the chilling clarity of an objective journalist, carefully avoiding the sentimentality or the nostalgia of a hometown boy."[27]

A Shrewd Analyst

The result of Baldwin's effort was an essay titled "The Harlem Ghetto," published in *Commentary* in February 1948. In the essay

Baldwin suggests that blacks, especially those who are strongly religious, identify with Jews in many ways:

> The more devout Negro considers that he is a Jew, in bondage to a hard taskmaster and waiting for a Moses to lead him out of Egypt. The hymns, the texts, and the most favored legends of the devout Negro are all Old Testament and therefore Jewish in origin.

Yet, Baldwin points out, Jews in Harlem were often businessmen, rent collectors, and pawn brokers; hence, they represent "the American business tradition of exploiting Negroes, and they are therefore hated for it." Furthermore, Baldwin suggests that many blacks feel that Jews, who were so often the target of prejudice, should have greater sympathy for African Americans: "An understanding is expected of the Jew such as none but the most naive and visionary Negro has ever expected of the American Gentile."[28]

Baldwin concludes his essay by stating that both "the Negro and Jew are helpless," that Jews have, unfortunately, become symbols of the black community's mistrust of white America. "But just as a society must have a scapegoat, so hatred must have a symbol. Georgia has the Negro and Harlem has the Jew."[29]

Because *Commentary* was a highly respected journal with a wide readership, "The Harlem Ghetto" earned Baldwin a national reputation as a shrewd analyst of America's racial tensions. Editors of other quality journals and magazines soon began to invite Baldwin to submit essays and reviews. He was still working at odd jobs to support himself, but he was establishing himself as a reviewer and essayist of great talent.

Jews and Blacks: Strained Relations

In "The Harlem Ghetto," an essay first published in Commentary *in February 1948, Baldwin commented on the strained relations between Jews and African Americans.*

"Both the Negro and the Jew are helpless; the pressure of living is too immediate and incessant to allow for understanding. I can conceive of no Negro native to this country who has not, by the age of puberty, been irreparably scarred by the conditions of his life. All over Harlem, Negro boys and girls are growing into stunted maturity, trying desperately to find a place to stand; and the wonder is not that so many are ruined but that so many survive. The Negro's outlets are desperately constricted. In his dilemma he turns first upon himself and then upon whatever most represents to him his own emasculation. Here the Jew is caught in the American crossfire. The Negro, facing a Jew, hates, at bottom, not his Jewishness but the color of his skin. It is not the Jewish tradition by which he has been betrayed but the tradition of his native land. But just as a society must have a scapegoat, so hatred must have a symbol. Georgia has the Negro and Harlem has the Jew."

Fiction, however, was always Baldwin's great love. He wanted to write like Dickens and Dostoyevsky, so while he completed the essays that he was commissioned to write, he also found time for fiction. He revised *Crying Holy* and began to work seriously on short stories. His first published piece of fiction, a short story titled "Previous Condition," appeared in *Commentary* in October 1948. The story concerned a struggling black actor who lived in Greenwich Village and his difficulty in finding a place in the white or black communities that surrounded him. When "Previous Condition" was published, the editors of *Commentary* heralded

Baldwin as "an important new talent on the literary scene."[30]

Despite these literary successes, Baldwin felt restless. He was becoming more and more disgusted with racial conditions in the United States. He felt the need to take some time away from the family that he had been trying to support since his stepfather's death. He needed time to read, reflect, and write. In the summer of 1947, Richard Wright left the United States to live in Paris, and a similar move seemed intriguing to Baldwin. So in November 1948, Baldwin was on an airplane heading for France, not knowing when or if he would return to his homeland.

3 A Writer in Paris

Since the Civil War, noteworthy American writers have been leaving their native soil for refuge in Paris. In 1875 Henry James, at age thirty-two, left New York for France to continue his great career as a novelist, essayist, and short story writer. After World War I, Ernest Hemingway, F. Scott Fitzgerald, and other writers who had grown into adulthood with the Great War departed the United States for Paris, a city that they found congenial for their literary endeavors. Richard Wright, one of James Baldwin's first literary mentors, left Brooklyn for Paris in 1947, and he resided there for the rest of his life.

Desperate to Leave

So when Baldwin boarded a plane for France in November 1948, he was following

Baldwin feared his own demise if he stayed in the United States. He could not tolerate the indignities of segregation and desperately hoped for a better life in Paris.

in the tradition of other expatriate American writers who believed that Paris would be the city to spur their literary imaginations. Baldwin did intend to write when he reached Paris, but he left the United States for a more basic reason. Discussing his departure many years later in an interview, Baldwin stated:

I had to get out of New York. . . . I knew what it meant to be white and I knew what it meant to be a nigger, and I knew what was going to happen to me. My luck was running out. I was going to go to jail, I was going to kill somebody or be killed. . . . It wasn't so much a matter of choosing France—it was a matter of getting out of America. I didn't know what was going to happen to me in France but I knew what was going to happen to me in New York. If I had stayed there, I would have gone under.[31]

He had already seen too many of the men with whom he had grown up go under. Ghetto life had broken their spirits and convinced them that they had no chance to improve their lives. Some were in prison, punished for street crimes. Others had taken to drugs or alcohol. One of Baldwin's close friends, a young black man named Eugene Worth, had become so despondent that he committed suicide

Reminders of America's racial segregation were everywhere— from hotels in the South to restaurants in the North. Baldwin sought relief in Paris from the oppressive atmosphere of segregation.

by jumping off the George Washington Bridge into the Hudson River. As David Leeming, the Baldwin biographer, states, "Eugene Worth had left New York by jumping into the Hudson River. Baldwin feared a similar fate. His flight to Paris was a desperate attempt to 'cheat the destruction' which he feared would be his fate in New York."[32]

Furthermore, the America that Baldwin was leaving in 1948 was a rigidly segregated society. In the South, blacks were prohibited by law from eating in some restaurants, lodging in certain hotels, and using public facilities such as parks and golf courses. Even in the North, Baldwin had sometimes experienced these kinds of indignities when he wanted to patronize a restaurant or business. Segregation of the races was widespread and accepted in the United States through the time of World War II. Baldwin believed that he might find more freedom in Paris than in his home country.

Life in Paris

James Baldwin arrived in Paris with only forty dollars in his pocket and of course, without a job. But Baldwin had survived the streets of Harlem, and he was confident that he could also navigate the avenues of Paris. He pawned his typewriter and borrowed money from people he had known in New York who had also resettled in Paris. Richard Wright was particularly helpful, lending Baldwin food money and setting him up in an inexpensive hotel.

Baldwin's relationship with Wright, however, soon soured. About six months after moving to Paris, Baldwin wrote an ar-

ticle for a new literary journal titled *Zero*. Baldwin's essay, "Everybody's Protest Novel," criticized American novels that were written as vehicles for social protest. Baldwin singled out two novels in his attack: Harriet Beecher Stowe's famous antislavery novel, *Uncle Tom's Cabin*, which Baldwin had so much enjoyed as a child, and Wright's powerful novel *Native Son*. Baldwin called *Uncle Tom's Cabin* "a very bad novel,"[33] and he criticized Wright's protagonist, Bigger Thomas, for being subhuman. Baldwin concluded his essay by asserting that the "failure of the protest novel lies in its rejection of life, the human being, the denial of his beauty, dread, power."[34]

Wright did not appreciate Baldwin's attack on his best novel and on protest literature in general, the kind of writing to which Wright had dedicated his life. On the day that Baldwin's article was published, Baldwin spotted Wright in a Paris cafe. The older writer called Baldwin over and blasted Baldwin for his article. "*All* literature is protest," claimed Wright. "You can't name a single novel that isn't protest."[35] But Baldwin stuck to his position, and the close friendship between the two writers ended.

Finding His Own Voice

Baldwin's attack on Wright, an established writer who had helped Baldwin advance his own career, might seem nasty and insensitive. To an extent it was. But in writing the article, Baldwin was playing the role of the brash young apprentice writer trying to move out from the shadow of his literary mentor. The twenty-four-year-old

Baldwin was trying to establish his own literary voice; he did not wish critics to view him as a literary descendant of Richard Wright. One way of avoiding that fate was to attack Wright's most famous novel. Baldwin later regretted losing Wright as a close friend; years later after Wright's death, Baldwin told Ellen Wright, the author's wife, and Julia Wright, his daughter, that he greatly admired Wright's work and that the strain in their relationship was somewhat exaggerated by others.

Baldwin's article was widely discussed in the literary circles in Paris, and it was reprinted in *Partisan Review*, a journal with a very large international audience. Thereafter, Baldwin received offers from the editors of other publications and earned much-needed funds.

A Chilling Experience

Still, however, life in Paris was a struggle for Baldwin. A little more than a year after he had moved to France, he was arrested and spent eight days in a Paris jail cell. The crime of which Baldwin was accused was the theft of a bedsheet. Actually, his friend had stolen a bedsheet from a hotel before checking out. When Baldwin complained that his own hotel rarely changed the bedsheets, his friend provided him

A Flight to Paris

In No Name in the Street, *a book-length autobiography published in 1972, James Baldwin explained why, as a young man, he had left New York for Paris.*

"My journey, or my flight, had not been *to* Paris, but simply *away* from America. For example, I had seriously considered going to work on a kibbutz in Israel, and I ended up in Paris almost literally by closing my eyes and putting my finger on a map. . . .

Still, my flight had been dictated by the hope that I could find myself in a place where I would be treated more humanely than my society had treated me at home, where my risks would be more personal, and my fate less austerely sealed. And Paris had done this for me: by leaving me completely alone. . . . I didn't want any help, and the French certainly didn't give me any—they let me do it myself; and for that reason, even knowing what I know, and unromantic as I am, there will always be a kind of love story between myself and that odd, unpredictable collection of bourgeois chauvinists who call themselves *la France.*"

Baldwin's relationship with writer Richard Wright (above) came to an end after Baldwin wrote an essay criticizing Wright's famous book Native Son.

with the clean, stolen sheet. When the chambermaid saw a sheet from another hotel on Baldwin's bed, she reported him to the police, and he was immediately arrested. He spent Christmas Day of 1949 in jail awaiting his trial, but in the courtroom two days after Christmas, all charges were dropped.

Nonetheless, the experience shook Baldwin emotionally. In an essay titled "Equal in Paris," published in *Harper's Magazine* five years after the bedsheet episode, Baldwin recorded what had been most upsetting about the incident. The announcement of Baldwin's acquittal had caused great laughter in the courtroom, but Baldwin reacted bitterly to the merriment:

I was chilled by their merriment in the courtroom though it was meant to warm me. It could only remind me of the laughter I had often heard at home. . . . This laughter is the laughter of those who consider themselves to be at a safe remove from all the wretched, for whom the pain of living is not real. I had heard it so often in my native land that I had resolved to find a place where I would never hear it any more. In some deep, black, stony, and liberating way, my life, in my own eyes, began during that first year in Paris, when it was borne in on me that this laughter is universal and never can be stilled.[36]

When he returned to his hotel after his release from jail, Baldwin attempted to hang himself with a dirty bedsheet. Fortunately, the water pipe to which Baldwin had attached the sheet broke. He quickly came to his senses, packed his bags, and checked out of the hotel. This was not the only time that Baldwin contemplated taking his own life. He considered it at other times, particularly when he felt lonely and friends were not close at hand. Fortunately, he always snapped out of his funk before taking any drastic action.

Literary Achievements

Despite poverty, imprisonment, the loss of his friend Richard Wright, and occasional loneliness, Baldwin survived in Paris. He made new friends, earned enough money to keep himself housed and fed, and learned the French language. More importantly, he returned to work on *Crying Holy*, his first novel.

Baldwin slowly began to revise the novel, renaming it *In My Father's House*. Late in 1951, however, he was frustrated with his progress and almost abandoned the project. His Paris friend, Lucien Happersberger, suggested that a change of locale might help, so Baldwin left Paris for a chalet owned by Happersberger's parents' in a small village in Switzerland.

Living alone in that Swiss village and working efficiently, Baldwin completed his manuscript in a few months. It was an autobiographical novel based on his family's life in the church, a book that Baldwin found painful to write because it made him confront so many of his past problems. Recalling his effort in an essay later published in *Nobody Knows My Name*, Baldwin stated, "There, in that alabaster landscape, armed with two Bessie Smith records and a typewriter, I began to re-create the life that I had first known as a child and from which I had spent years in flight."[37]

Baldwin's First Novel

When he finished the book, renamed *Go Tell It on the Mountain*, Baldwin returned to Paris and sent the manuscript to Helen Strauss, who was serving as his literary agent. In a short time, Strauss informed Baldwin that the Alfred A. Knopf publishing company was interested in purchasing his novel. The editors wanted to meet him in New York and discuss further revisions.

In February 1952 Baldwin returned to New York for the first time in more than three years. The editors at Knopf offered him a modest contract for his first novel: Baldwin would receive $250 immediately; and he would receive an additional $750

when the revisions were completed and the novel was ready for publication. Baldwin agreed and returned to France to work on the revisions and await publication.

Go Tell It on the Mountain, which appeared in the spring of 1953, tells the story of the Grimes family, an African American family living in Harlem during the 1930s. The novel's protagonist, fourteen-year-old John Grimes, is trying to cope with his harsh, sometimes abusive father and attempting to hold onto his religious beliefs despite the temptations of the world. Early in the novel as John watches a movie (entertainment strictly forbidden by his stern father), he

> struggled to find a compromise between the way that led to life everlasting and the way that ended in the pit. But there was none. . . . Either he arose from this theater, never to re-

Baldwin returned to New York in February 1952 after receiving a contract to publish his first novel, Go Tell It on the Mountain. *Here, Baldwin poses years later with a copy of his acclaimed novel.*

Baldwin's First Novel

The opening paragraphs of Go Tell It on the Mountain *reveal that Baldwin's first novel was autobiographical.*

"Everyone had always said that John would be a preacher when he grew up, just like his father. It had been said so often that John, without ever thinking about it, had come to believe it himself. Not until the morning of his fourteenth birthday did he really begin to think about it, and by then it was already too late.

His earliest memories—which were in a way, his only memories—were of the hurry and brightness of Sunday mornings. They all rose together on that day; his father, who did not have to go to work, and led them in prayer before breakfast; his mother, who dressed up on that day, and looked almost young, with her hair straightened, and on her head the close-fitting white cap that was the uniform of holy women; his younger brother, Roy, who was silent that day because his father was home. Sarah, who wore a red ribbon in her hair that day, and was fondled by her father. And the baby, Ruth, who was dressed in pink and white, and rode in her mother's arms to church."

---

turn, putting behind him the world and its pleasures, its honors, and its glories, or he remained here with the wicked and partook of their certain punishment.[38]

John's father, Gabriel Grimes, is based on Baldwin's own stepfather. He is a harsh, often cruel man. Baldwin recounts the tragedies of Gabriel's life and urges the reader to understand this flawed character, and perhaps sympathize with him, just as Baldwin had struggled to understand David Baldwin. The other members of the Grimes family, John's mother, brother, and aunt, are also sensitively de-

picted, making the novel a tender fictional portrait of Baldwin's own family.

Go Tell It on the Mountain concludes with John Grimes's religious conversion during a church service, an event similar to the one that Baldwin himself had experienced as a teenager. In stirring, eloquent prose Baldwin describes John's religious rebirth:

Yes, the night had passed, the powers of darkness had been beaten back. He moved among the saints, he John, who had come home, who was one of their company now; weeping, he yet could find no words to speak of his great gladness; and he scarcely knew how he

In his review in the New York Times, Orville Prescott compared James Baldwin's first novel to Invisible Man, *the 1952 masterpiece by African American writer Ralph Ellison.*

"James Baldwin, like Johnny [Grimes], is the son of a Harlem preacher. Although he is only 29 years old, he is a sound craftsman in fiction. As individually and authentically talented as Ralph Ellison, author of last year's 'The Invisible Man,' Mr. Baldwin has made an equally auspicious debut. Readers interested in Negro fiction, an increasingly large number, will not want to miss 'Go Tell It on the Mountain.'. . .

With vivid imagery, with lavish attention to all the details of the Harlem scene and with much eloquent dialogue (colloquial but not so extreme as to seem a dialect), Mr. Baldwin has told his feverish story, using flashback with great skill to transport his characters into the far past in the nameless community of their origin somewhere in the South."

moved, for his hands were new, and his feet were new, and he moved in a new and Heaven-bright air. Praying Mother Washington took him in her arms, and kissed him, and their tears, his tears and the tears of the old, black woman, mingled.[39]

The novel's ending is hopeful: John is optimistic that he has been saved from the evil around him, just as Baldwin survived the temptations of his own youth. The novel's dedication to both his mother and father suggests, perhaps, that Baldwin had begun to understand and forgive his stepfather.

Baldwin's first novel received excellent reviews. Writing in the *New York Times Book Review*, Donald Barr described *Go Tell It on the Mountain* as a "beautiful, furious first novel."[40] Other reviewers were equally enthusiastic. Even Richard Wright, whose friendship with Baldwin had ended by this time, spoke highly of his former friend's first novel. Baldwin was delighted. He had struggled with the book for almost ten years. Encouraged by his success, he began planning other writing projects—a second novel, essays, a play.

A Most Productive Time

The three years after the publication of *Go Tell It on the Mountain* were among Baldwin's most productive. In 1954 he completed his first play, *The Amen Corner*, which also was based on his boyhood religious experiences. The play's main character, Sister Margaret, resembles Mother Horn, the dynamic minister he had met in Harlem as a youngster. In May 1955 the theater department at Howard University produced the play, and Baldwin traveled to Washington, D.C., to see it performed. Audiences and reviewers approved, and Baldwin was awarded a prestigious Guggenheim Fellowship based on the success of his first novel and play. The Guggenheim Fellowships are financial grants awarded to Americans engaging in noteworthy scholarly or creative endeavors. The award was evidence that at age thirty-one Baldwin was already recognized as a writer of great merit.

In 1955 Baldwin collected ten of his essays, added a short autobiographical introduction, and published the works under the title *Notes of a Native Son*, his first volume of essays. Although all of the essays contained in the book had appeared earlier in magazines and journals, the collection presented Baldwin's work to readers who did not subscribe to these publications. *Notes of a Native Son* is a good introduction to Baldwin as an essayist. The collection includes essays on his Harlem youth, on his life in Paris, and on racial issues. Langston Hughes, the great African American poet, reviewed the book for the *New York Times*. He criticized Baldwin for viewing life through the lens of race

The Amen Corner, *Baldwin's first play, was received warmly by both audiences and reviewers. Baldwin is pictured here at a 1965 production with producer Mrs. Nat Cole (left) and star Bea Richards.*

An Act of Desperation

"In his room he tied one of the original dirty sheets to a water pipe, stood on a chair, tied the loose end of the sheet around his neck, and jumped. The only thing that gave way was the water pipe. The hanging had been a desperate act of solidarity with all of those literally and metaphorically imprisoned 'blacks' of all races who must bear the agony of not being recognized as human beings. By means of it, the tension and the depression were broken. Rebaptized by the flood of water from the broken pipe, he found himself overcome by a kind of laughter that was more powerful than the laughter in court. He threw some clothes in a duffel bag and rushed down the stairs into the bright streets. He never returned to the Hotel du Bac."

rather than looking at life "purely as himself, and for himself, the color of his skin mattering not at all." But Hughes acknowledged that "Few American writers handle words more effectively in the essay form than James Baldwin."[41]

During this time Baldwin also worked hard on his second novel, *Giovanni's Room.* He had difficulty finding a publisher for this book because its subject matter was considered taboo at the time. The novel's main character, David, is a young man struggling to accept his homosexuality. The novel revolves around David's relationship with a homosexual Parisian bartender named Giovanni and ends tragically, with David rejecting Giovanni and Giovanni committing a murder for which he is convicted and sentenced to death.

Giovanni's Room is one of the first serious novels by an American writer to con-

Poet Langston Hughes (pictured) criticized Baldwin's Notes of a Native Son *for its narrow focus on race but praised Baldwin's gift for expression in the essay form.*

The literary world honored Baldwin in 1956 when it awarded him a Partisan Review Fellowship and the prestigious National Institute of Arts and Letters Award.

front homosexuality. Helen Strauss, Baldwin's agent, suggested that he burn the manuscript to protect his reputation. She reasoned that if publishers suspected that Baldwin was homosexual, then they might be wary of publishing any future Baldwin book, whether or not it dealt with homosexuality. Baldwin, who had romantic relationships with both men and women during his lifetime, rejected his agent's advice. But Dial Press accepted *Giovanni's Room* and courageously published it late in 1956. Reviews of the novel, not surprisingly, were mixed, with some reviewers condemning the book's controversial subject matter and others applauding Baldwin's ability to treat a taboo subject with genuine sensitivity.

More Accolades

Besides the publication of *Giovanni's Room*, Baldwin celebrated two other signif-

icant achievements in 1956. He received a Partisan Review Fellowship, a financial grant awarded to young writers of merit by the publishers of the *Partisan Review*, a highly regarded literary journal. Baldwin also received the prestigious National Institute of Arts and Letters Award, conferred upon writers and artists who had produced a body of impressive work. The National Institute recognized Baldwin "for the excellent directness of his prose style and for the combination of objectivity and passion with which he approaches his subject matter."[42]

Baldwin had moved to Paris in 1948 to escape the racism he faced in America and to write. He had accomplished both goals. In Paris he had escaped temporarily the overt racism that he encountered every day in the United States, and by age thirty-two he had created an impressive body of literary works. He had become an accomplished writer with an international audience.

4 An Exile's Return

While James Baldwin was living in Paris, great changes were taking place in the United States in the area of race relations. In effect, a revolution was occurring.

In April 1947, the year before Baldwin moved to France, Jackie Robinson donned a Brooklyn Dodgers uniform and played in his first big league game, breaking major league baseball's color barrier. A year later President Harry Truman integrated the U.S. armed forces, which had previously mandated separate regiments for white and black servicemen. During the 1950s more dramatic changes would occur.

In 1954 in a unanimous decision, the U.S. Supreme Court outlawed school segregation in *Brown v. Board of Education*. Chief Justice Earl Warren, explaining the Court's decision, stated that "in the field of public education 'separate but equal' has no place. Separate educational facilities are inherently unequal."[43] This case, which was argued on behalf of the National Association for the Advancement of Colored People (NAACP) by a young lawyer named Thurgood Marshall (later to be the first African American Supreme Court justice), gave opponents of racial segregation a legal precedent on which to carry their cause: If segregation had no place in public schools, then perhaps it had no place anywhere in America.

The Long March

The Civil Rights movement had begun. One of the movement's first victories took place in Montgomery, Alabama, where a black seamstress named Rosa Parks disobeyed a local ordinance that required her to surrender her bus seat to a white passenger if another seat was not available. She was arrested and fined fourteen dollars for breaking the law, but her community's black leaders took up her cause, urging African American citizens to boycott the buses until the discriminatory bus-seating laws were repealed. The boycott lasted more than a year, at which time the Supreme Court ruled Montgomery's bus-seating laws unconstitutional.

The Montgomery bus boycott was led by an inspirational young clergyman named Martin Luther King Jr. Spurred on by his victory in Montgomery, Reverend King began to carry his message calling for an end to racial segregation throughout the South. With fiery, eloquent speeches, he urged Americans, both black and white, to work to create a fully integrated society. Inspired by King, Americans from both the North and South began demanding that their lawmakers enact legislation to outlaw discrimination

Respect for the Victims of Segregation

In The Fire Next Time, *published in 1963, James Baldwin eloquently pays homage to southern blacks who have suffered the indignities of segregation with fortitude and dignity.*

"It demands great force and great cunning continually to assault the mighty and indifferent fortress of white supremacy, as Negroes in this country have done so long. It demands great spiritual resilience not to hate the hater whose foot is on your neck, and an even greater miracle of perception and charity not to teach your child to hate. The Negro boys and girls who are facing mobs today come out of a long line of improbable aristocrats—the only genuine aristocrats this country has produced. . . . They were hewing out of the mountain of white supremacy the stone of their individuality. I have great respect for that unsung army of black men and women who trudged down back lanes and entered back doors, saying 'Yes, sir' and 'No, Ma'am' in order to acquire a new roof for the schoolhouse, new books, a new chemistry lab, more beds for the dormitories, more dormitories. They did not like saying 'Yes, sir' and 'No, Ma'am,' but the country was in no hurry to educate Negroes, these black men and women knew that the job had to be done, and they put their pride in their pockets in order to do it."

in all forms. During the mid-1950s, America marched unevenly down the road toward a fully integrated society.

A Native Son Comes Home

James Baldwin was still living in Paris and working on his first significant literary achievements when the Civil Rights movement began to gain momentum in his homeland. Although he had kept abreast of racial developments in the United

States, he felt somewhat divorced from them. His journey to Paris had been an attempt to find a personal peace; rather than work to correct the injustices to which he and other African Americans were subjected, Baldwin had chosen to escape those hardships by living on a different continent. In 1948 that seemed to be a wise choice for Baldwin. He firmly believed that if he had stayed in the United States much longer, he would have ended up in prison or dead in some Harlem alleyway.

But by the fall of 1956, Baldwin had begun to question his decision to live in

Baldwin's move to Paris had been an attempt to find personal peace, but as the Civil Rights movement progressed he began to reconsider his absence from the United States.

exile. He missed his mother and siblings and worried about their well-being. He was also very much encouraged by the great changes in the area of race relations that were taking place at home, and he wanted to be a part of them. He began to make tentative plans to return to America.

The event that finally prompted Baldwin's return to the United States occurred during an international conference of black writers and artists that was held in Paris that fall. During a conference lunch break, Baldwin purchased a newspaper whose front page showed a photograph of Dorothy Counts, a fifteen-year-old high school student from Charlotte, North Carolina. Dorothy was one of the first black students to integrate her local high school, and the photo showed her walking into the school building with great pride and dignity while white students stood by spitting at her and shouting insults.

The photograph and the accompanying news story moved Baldwin. He had heard of the Supreme Court's desegregation ruling, but he had not considered its impact and importance until he saw the photograph of Dorothy Counts. He later wrote about the incident:

> It made me furious, it filled me with both hatred and pity, and it made me ashamed. . . . Some of us should have been there with her! . . . I could, simply, no longer sit around in Paris discussing the . . . black American problem. Everyone else was paying their dues, and it was time I went home and paid mine.[44]

Baldwin stayed in Paris for several more months. In the summer of 1957, he headed back to the United States with the specific purpose of going to the South to experience America's civil rights battles firsthand. He had been away a long time, and he had missed a lot.

Journeying South

Baldwin returned to America in July 1957. He spent a few weeks in New York visiting old friends and family. He had particularly missed his younger brothers and sisters. "I missed my brothers especially," he later wrote, "missed David's grin and George's solemnity and Wilmer's rages, missed, in

A Letter from the South

James Baldwin ends his essay "A Letter from the South" with a penetrating analysis of America's racial problem. The essay was written after Baldwin's tour of the South in 1957 and published in Nobody Knows My Name.

"What it comes to, finally, is that the nation has spent a large part of its time and energy looking away from one of the principal facts of its life. This failure to look reality in the face diminishes a nation as it diminishes a person, and it can only be described as unmanly. . . . Any honest examination of the national life proves how far we are from the standard of human freedom with which we began. The recovery of this standard demands of everyone who loves this country a hard look at himself, for the greatest achievements must begin somewhere, and they always begin with the person. If we are not capable of this examination, we may yet become one of the most distinguished and monumental failures in the history of nations."

A photo and news account of Dorothy Counts (pictured), one of the first black students to integrate her high school in Charlotte, North Carolina, prompted Baldwin's return to the United States.

short, my connections, missed the life which had produced me and nourished me and paid for me."[45]

But Baldwin did not return to America for a family reunion; he came home for political reasons—to experience for himself the dramatic changes that had been taking place in the United States as the Civil Rights movement gained momentum and, of course, to write about what he saw. The best place for Baldwin to see what was happening in his country was not in New York City but in the South, and that is where his investigation began.

Baldwin had never visited the South. Some of his slave ancestors had left the South to find their freedom north of the Mason-Dixon line; his mother and stepfather were southerners who left their home region to find justice and opportunity in the North. Now Baldwin was making that journey in reverse—leaving New York and journeying south to experience firsthand the struggles that southern blacks faced as they attempted to rid their region of segregation. For Baldwin, the South was, as he later put it, "territory absolutely hostile and exceedingly strange."[46]

Firsthand Views

Baldwin's first stop was Charlotte, North Carolina, where Dorothy Counts had bravely attempted to integrate her local high school in the face of hateful opposition. There he saw the damaging effects of segregated schools. "I saw the Negro schools in Charlotte," he later wrote, "saw on street corners, several of their alumnae, and read about others who had been sentenced to the chain gang."[47] He understood why the parents of black students wanted so badly to send their children to white schools, even if it meant subjecting the youngsters to violent mobs of protesters. He later wrote:

They are doing it because they want the child to receive the education which will allow him to defeat, possibly escape, and not impossibly help one day abolish the stifling environment in which they see, daily, so many children perish.[48]

Young Klan members and supporters of segregation peer out of their car window during a Ku Klux Klan rally. After witnessing racism in the South, Baldwin described the region as "absolutely hostile and exceedingly strange."

Reverend King at Work

In an essay on Martin Luther King Jr., written for Harper's Magazine, *James Baldwin describes the great civil rights leader leading a church service in his Montgomery church and his congregation focusing on each of his words.*

"And, surely, very few people had ever spoken to them as King spoke. King is a great speaker. The secret of his greatness does not lie in his voice or his presence or his manner, though it has something to do with all of these; nor does it lie in his verbal range or felicity, which are not striking; nor does he have any capacity for those stunning, demagogic flights of the imagination which bring an audience cheering to its feet. The secret lies, I think, in his intimate knowledge of the people he is addressing, be they black or white, and in the forthrightness with which he speaks of those things which hurt and baffle them. He does not offer any easy comfort and this keeps his hearers absolutely tense. He allows them their self-respect—indeed, he insists on it.

'We know,' he told them, 'that there are many things wrong in the white world. But there are many things wrong in the black world, too. We can't keep blaming the white man. There are many things we must do for ourselves.'"

Martin Luther King Jr. deeply inspired and impressed Baldwin on their first meeting. The friendship that developed between the two men lasted until King's death.

Baldwin's next stop was Atlanta, where he experienced the honor of meeting Martin Luther King Jr. for the first time and the dishonor of riding his first segregated bus. His meeting with King, in a hotel room, was brief because King was working hard to finish a book and was seeing few visitors. Baldwin was much impressed by the great civil rights leader. In an article on the meeting in *Harper's Magazine*, Baldwin described King as "immediately and tremendously winning," a man with "an inquiring and genuine smile on his face."[49] The brief encounter began a friendship that lasted until King's death a decade later.

From Atlanta, Baldwin traveled to Montgomery, the scene of the successful bus boycott of the previous year. In Montgomery, Baldwin attended one of King's Sunday services, which "transcended anything I have ever felt in a church before."[50] That highlight, however, was almost negated by an experience he had walking the streets of Montgomery on a pleasant late-summer evening.

That evening, around suppertime, Baldwin left his hotel for a stroll through town. After walking through a black neighborhood, he spotted a restaurant a block away. He entered the eatery, intending to take a seat and order his dinner. He later described what occurred when he set foot inside the restaurant:

Every white face turned to stone: the arrival of the messenger of death could not have had a more devastating effect than the appearance in the restaurant of a small, unarmed, utterly astounded black man. I had realized my error as soon as I opened the door: but the absolute terror on all these white faces—I swear that not a soul moved—paralyzed me. They stared at me, I stared at them.[51]

Baldwin had walked into a whites-only restaurant. Quickly, he backed out the door. A white man standing in front of the restaurant sensed Baldwin's error and pointed to a side door. Baldwin entered and found himself in a small cubicle equipped with a counter and stools; it was in the back of the restaurant. Through a mesh screen he ordered a hamburger and coffee. The burger was wrapped in paper, and the coffee was served in a paper cup, presumably so that the restaurant staff would not have to wash the dishes off which black people ate.

Courage and Dignity

Demeaning incidents like this one, however, were offset by the moving examples of courage and dignity that Baldwin witnessed as he journeyed throughout the South. He later wrote that "so many of the black men I talked to in the South in those years were—I can find no other word for them—heroic." He found their heroism not in great public demonstrations but in small, private ones: "What impressed me was how they went about their daily tasks in the teeth of Southern terror."[52]

Baldwin offered as an example the Reverend Fred Shuttlesworth, pastor of the First Baptist Church in Birmingham, Alabama. While Baldwin was visiting that city, Shuttlesworth, who was in the vanguard of the efforts to end segregation in Birmingham, visited him in his hotel room one night. Baldwin stated that Shuttlesworth "was a marked man in Birmingham."[53] Civil rights advocates in the South were often the targets of acts of violence and even death threats delivered by hostile white citizens who wanted the walls of segregation to remain firmly in place. While the two men talked in Baldwin's room, Shuttlesworth kept looking out the window, eyeing his car, making sure (Baldwin reasoned) that no one placed a bomb in it. When the pastor left the hotel late at night, Baldwin urged him to be careful. Shuttlesworth simply smiled and with "no hint of defiance or bravado in his manner"[54] walked across the parking lot, started his car, and drove off alone into the night.

Baldwin also traveled to Little Rock, Arkansas, where nine black students were attempting to integrate Central High School. Because Little Rock's white citizens were so hostile and abusive to the school's new African American students, President Dwight Eisenhower was forced to dispatch federal troops, the 101st Airborne Division, to protect the students while they attended classes. Once again, Baldwin was impressed with the way that the black students conducted themselves in such a difficult situation.

Federal troops were called in to protect nine black students who were attempting to integrate Central High School in Little Rock, Arkansas. Baldwin visited Little Rock during this time and was impressed with the way the black students handled themselves.

Brown v. Board of Education

The 1954 Brown v. Board of Education of Topeka, Kansas, *Supreme Court decision outlawed segregation in public schools. The decision was later cited as evidence that segregation in all public places is unconstitutional. The Court's opinion was written by Chief Justice Earl Warren.*

"Today, education is perhaps the most important function of state and local governments. Compulsory school attendance laws and the great expenditures for education both demonstrate our recognition of the importance of education to our democratic society. It is required in the performance of our most basic public responsibilities, even service in the armed forces. It is the very foundation of good citizenship. Today it is a principal instrument in awakening the child to cultural values, in preparing him for later professional training, and helping him to adjust normally to his environment. In these days, it is doubtful that any child may reasonably be expected to succeed in life if he is denied the opportunity of an education. Such an opportunity, where the state has undertaken to provide it, is a right which must be made available to all on equal terms."

A group of black students on their way to class at a southern high school pass demonstrators carrying signs urging segregation. The Brown v. Board of Education *Supreme Court decision outlawed segregation in public schools.*

A courtroom scene from the Emmett Till murder trial (left). Civil rights leader Medgar Evers (below) told Baldwin what had happened during the trial.

An Appalling Tale

Baldwin visited several Mississippi towns. In Jackson he met a young civil rights leader named Medgar Evers, who filled Baldwin in on the details of the murder of Emmett Till, a fourteen-year-old African American boy from Chicago who had been murdered while visiting relatives in Mississippi in 1955. Emmett had whistled at an attractive white woman, and her husband and another man had kidnapped and brutally murdered the youngster to punish him for his action. The two men were later acquitted by an all-white jury.

Baldwin was appalled by this horrid tale, and remembered the story for a long time. Eventually, he used the broad outline of the Till murder to create his second play, *Blues for Mister Charlie*. Its main character, Richard Henry, is a young African American who returns to the South after having lived in New York for

several years. Unwilling to suffer the indignities heaped upon southern blacks, Richard becomes active in the town's fledgling Civil Rights movement. When he angers Lyle, a local store owner, Lyle kills Richard. Like the murderers of Emmett

Blues from Mr. Baldwin

In the climax of James Baldwin's play Blues for Mister Charlie, *Lyle tells his wife, Jo, why he killed a young black man. Lyle's confession follows his acquittal by a jury.*

"LYLE: I had to kill him. I'm a white man! Can't nobody talk that way to *me!* I had to go and get my pick-up truck and load him in it—I had to carry him on my back—and carry him out to the high weeds. And I dumped him in the weeds, face down. And then I come on home, to my good Jo here.

JO: Come on, Lyle. We got to get on home. We got to get the little one home now.

LYLE: And I ain't sorry. I want you to know that I ain't sorry!

JO: Come on, Lyle. Come on. He's hungry. I got to feed him."

The proud playwright is pictured here at the opening of his play, Blues for Mr. Charlie, *with actress Diana Sands and director Burgess Meredith.*

Till, Lyle is acquitted by an all-white jury, and the white townspeople applaud the decision. *Blues for Mister Charlie* was produced on Broadway in 1964.

What Baldwin saw on his tour of the South both horrified and energized him. He witnessed and heard of terrible injustices that had to be stopped. He encountered scores of heroes who fought injustice with courage and dignity, people who needed his support and encouragement. Having experienced the civil rights battles firsthand, Baldwin realized that he could no longer play the role of a detached observer, discoursing upon American racial issues from Paris cafes. He needed to take a more active part in the great events that were changing his country. As one of Baldwin's biographers later put it, "As much as it was a magazine assignment, this first journey to the South was a voyage of discovery and a rite of initiation." [55]

Chapter

5 The Writer as Political Activist

After his tour of the South in 1957, Baldwin traveled elsewhere in the United States. Then late in 1959, feeling somewhat restless, he returned to Paris. Although he had been encouraged by the changes that were taking place in the United States, Baldwin still felt the need to escape his homeland on occasion and take a break from the events that were reshaping America. During the next several years, he became a Paris-to-New-York "commuter," living in Paris for long stretches of time but returning home for extended visits. He also journeyed to Spain, to Istanbul, and made his first trip to Africa.

Despite his extensive travels, Baldwin remained committed to the Civil Rights movement that was taking place in the United States. After touring the South and meeting Martin Luther King Jr. and other civil rights activists, Baldwin could no longer observe what was happening from the distant safety of his Paris apartment; he needed to become politically involved in a more direct way. Looking back on that time in a later interview, he stated:

Once I was in the civil rights milieu, once I'd met Martin Luther King, Jr. and Malcolm X and Medgar Evers and all those other people, the role I had to play was confirmed. I didn't think

of myself as a public speaker, or as a spokesman, but I knew I could get a story past the editor's desk. And once you realize that you can do something, it would be difficult to live with yourself if you didn't do it.[56]

He had accepted the role of political activist. He performed his role best at the typewriter, articulating civil rights issues in moving and eloquent prose. But Baldwin often stepped away from his desk to involve himself directly in some of the dramatic civil rights events that took place during the 1960s.

Speaking and Marching

In the summer of 1960, Baldwin joined the Congress of Racial Equality (CORE), an organization that had been promoting civil rights since the early 1940s. The leaders of CORE, the NAACP, and other civil rights groups welcomed Baldwin into their ranks. They had read his novels and essays and were enthusiastic about his more direct involvement with the Civil Rights movement.

At that time CORE was sponsoring a series of sit-ins at restaurants in the South

(Left) Two black students take part in an organized protest against segregation by sitting in a Raleigh, North Carolina, restaurant that caters only to whites. Baldwin became an active member of the organization CORE, which sponsored protests like this one. (Below) Here, Baldwin speaks on the group's behalf.

that were still refusing to serve black patrons. Typically, a dozen or so CORE members would sit at the counter of a segregated diner and refuse to leave when ordered to do so. They were insulted, beaten, and arrested, but little by little, southern restaurants and lunch counters were integrated. In August 1960 Baldwin traveled from Paris to Tallahassee, Florida, to participate in CORE's strategy session on coordinating the sit-ins and orchestrating a nationwide boycott of restaurant chains that refused to serve black customers.

Thereafter Baldwin, when he was not writing, became very active in CORE-sponsored events, speaking at its conferences and rallies around the United States. Early in 1963 CORE arranged a speaking tour for Baldwin that took him to more than a dozen southern cities. Addressing crowds in auditoriums and churches, Baldwin spread the new gospel of civil rights to his listeners. He relied on the same techniques that he had used as a teenager preaching in Harlem's storefront churches. He never wrote out or memorized a speech. He prepared a few general points in his mind, then spoke impromptu when he reached the podium. Baldwin's appearances attracted large audiences as well as the media. On May 17, 1963, Baldwin's picture adorned the cover of *Time* magazine; a week later his CORE-sponsored speaking tour was *Life* magazine's feature story.

It was through CORE that Baldwin became involved in the March on Washington for jobs and freedom in the summer of 1963. Throughout that spring CORE, the NAACP, the Southern Christian Leadership Conference, and other civil rights groups had been planning a massive march to Washington, an opportunity for African Americans to take their desire for an end to segregation and the economic inequities that went along with it to their nation's capital.

On August 28, 1963, more than 200,000 people from around the country traveled to Washington and gathered in the area around the Lincoln Memorial to hear a series of speakers address the civil rights issues of the day. Folksingers Joan Baez and Peter, Paul, and Mary entertained the group with stirring anthems. The keynote speaker was Martin Luther King Jr., who delivered the speech for which he is best known—"I Have a Dream."

King began by outlining the promises of freedom guaranteed by the nation's founders in the Declaration of Independence and Constitution. Then he sadly noted that the country had yet to extend these guarantees to its citizens of color. In stirring, eloquent language he called on all

Baldwin the Speaker

In The Furious Passage of James Baldwin, *Fern Marja Eckman describes Baldwin's speaking style. Baldwin is addressing a crowd gathered in the Community Church of New York.*

"What he says is now drenched with the naked intensity that is Baldwin's style—in writing, in talking, in living. His words are delivered at an uneven pace, sometimes with a rush, sometimes with long, brooding intervals. His voice, resonant, a bit theatrical, with a hint of the vaulted intonation good English actors often have, slurs a little when he reaches a climax, compressing a phrase into a single vibrant syllable.

In the course of the next half hour, he unfurls the broad canvas of inequality that is the Negro's lot in the United States. He calls for a rent moratorium to prod Harlem's landlords into repairing slum tenements. He advocates the use of American industrial and commercial power—the power generated by the sweat of black men—'for ourselves and the liberation of this country.' He says, 'We are responsible for our own freedom; we are not *begging* for it.'"

Thousands of people, Baldwin among them, turned out for the March on Washington on August 28, 1963. The demonstration invigorated Baldwin and other marchers and raised hopes for a truly egalitarian society.

citizens to end the discrimination that was preventing his country from becoming a great nation. And King ended with an assertion of hope. "I have a dream," he repeated again and again, "that one day this nation will rise up and live out the true meaning of its creed—we hold these truths to be self-evident, that all men are created equal"; that "the sons of former slaves and the sons of former slave-owners will be able to sit down together at the table of brotherhood"; that his own children "will one day live in a nation where they will not be judged by the color of their skin but by the content of their character."[57]

For Baldwin the march had begun in Paris. A week before the Washington gathering, Baldwin had marched from the American Church in Paris to the American embassy with a petition bearing one thousand names and demanding equal rights for black Americans. He was in Washington for the great march and rally. Baldwin, the actors Sidney Poitier and Charlton Heston, and the entertainer Harry Belafonte were preparing to tape a

"I Have a Dream"

Martin Luther King Jr., speaking from the Lincoln Memorial before a crowd of 200,000 people on August 28, 1963, delivered his famous "I Have a Dream" speech, which put into eloquent words the hope of all who worked tirelessly in the Civil Rights movement. King concludes the speech with these stirring words.

"So let freedom ring from the prodigious hilltops of New Hampshire.

Let freedom ring from the mighty mountains of New York.

Let freedom ring from the heightening Alleghenies of Pennsylvania.

Let freedom ring from the snow-capped Rockies of Colorado.

Let freedom ring from the curvaceous slopes of California.

But not only that.

Let freedom ring from Stone Mountain of Georgia.

Let freedom ring from Lookout Mountain of Tennessee.

Let freedom ring from every hill and molehill of Mississippi, from every mountainside, let freedom ring.

And when we allow freedom to ring, when we let it ring from every village and hamlet, from every state and city, we will be able to speed up the day when all of God's children—black men and white men, Jews and Gentiles, Catholics and Protestants—will be able to join hands and to sing the words of the old Negro spiritual, 'Free at last, free at last; thank God Almighty, we are free at last.'"

Martin Luther King Jr. delivers his stirring "I Have a Dream" speech at the March on Washington.

Voice of America radio program about the march when King delivered his famous speech, so they watched the great orator on television. Baldwin later put into writing the feeling of hope that he had after hearing King's moving words:

> That day, for a moment, it almost seemed that we stood on a height, and could see our inheritance; perhaps we could make the kingdom real, perhaps the beloved community would not forever remain that dream one dreamed in agony.[58]

The historic March on Washington provided the energy that led to the passage of the Civil Rights Act of 1964. That act, signed into law by President Lyndon Johnson on July 2, 1964, outlawed discrimination in public places such as hotels, restaurants, and theaters. It became one of the most important pieces of legislation passed during the Civil Rights movement.

Another great victory of the Civil Rights movement came after another famous march in which Baldwin took part. In March 1965 Martin Luther King Jr. and other civil rights leaders planned a march from Selma to Montgomery, Alabama, to demand that voting rights be extended to that state's black citizens. Alabama's citizens of color were often intimidated and threatened with loss of jobs and loss of limbs when they went to city hall to register to vote. Voter registrants were given difficult tests to pass before being allowed to register, or they were ordered to pay a stiff "poll tax" before voting.

The fifty-mile march from Selma to Montgomery began on Sunday, March 7, after a church service, but the marchers were intimidated and beaten by state troopers and Ku Klux Klansmen, so they

President Lyndon Johnson signs into law the Civil Rights Act of 1964, the landmark legislation that outlawed discrimination in all public places.

turned back. One marcher was killed; many others were injured. Finally, President Johnson guaranteed the safety of the marchers by providing protection by the National Guard, and the marchers began again. On March 21 thousands of marchers, Baldwin included, marched on Alabama's capitol building, where King made a stirring speech demanding that American citizens of color be allowed to exercise their constitutional right to vote. That same week, President Johnson asked Congress to pass a strong voting rights act, and that act became law on August 6, 1965.

Tragedies—Personal and Political

Despite these great victories, the Civil Rights movement experienced a number of setbacks and tragedies during the 1960s. Because Baldwin had worked so closely with the movement's leaders, many of these tragedies were very personal.

The first was the murder of Medgar Evers, an NAACP leader in Mississippi and friend of Baldwin, who was shot by a white racist outside his own home on June 12, 1963. Baldwin later wrote of Evers's death that he had "been haunted by it often."[59] He had been fond of Evers and his family; Baldwin had lost a friend, and the Civil Rights movement had lost a great leader. The murder of Evers also made Baldwin fear for his own life. Like Evers, Baldwin was a public figure, and he wondered whether another white racist would take aim at him one day.

Another tragedy occurred at a Birmingham church less than three weeks after the successful March on Washington. On September 15, 1963 a bomb was set off at that church during a Sunday school program, and four young African American girls were killed in the explosion. King,

The fifty-mile march from Selma to Montgomery, Alabama, attracted thousands of people. Baldwin (far left), singer Joan Baez, and James Forman, chairman of SNCC, link hands as they make their way along the route.

Less than three weeks after the March on Washington, four young black girls were killed when a bomb was set off at a Birmingham church. Here, marchers protest the tragic deaths.

delivering the eulogy at the girls' funeral, hoped that "the spilt blood of these innocent girls may cause the whole citizenry of Birmingham to transform the negative extremes of a dark past into the positive extremes of a bright future,"[60] but this tragedy was a harbinger of tragedies to come.

On February 21, 1965, the Black Muslim leader Malcolm X was assassinated during a rally in New York City. Baldwin had met Malcolm X, and though he often disagreed with the Muslim leader, Baldwin respected him greatly. Malcolm X was a separatist, believing that America's black people would fare far better politically and economically if they separated themselves from white America. Unlike King, who preached nonviolence, Malcolm X called on blacks to arm themselves to defend against white oppression. Earlier in his career, the Black Muslims had courted Baldwin; Baldwin had declined to join them. But he respected Malcolm X enough to make him the subject of a

Malcolm X, shown here before his assassination. Baldwin did not agree with the Black Muslim leader's separatist views but still respected him.

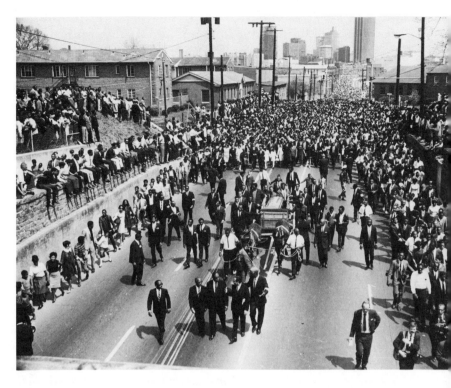

The mule-drawn casket of Martin Luther King Jr. leads thousands of mourners through the streets of Atlanta. King's murder devastated the Civil Rights movement and left Baldwin feeling bitter and disheartened.

screenplay after the assassination. The project was never turned into a movie, but it was published in book form in 1972 under the title *One Day, When I Was Lost*.

The greatest blow, both to the Civil Rights movement and to James Baldwin personally, occurred on April 4, 1968. On that day Martin Luther King Jr. was murdered outside his hotel room in Memphis, Tennessee, where he had spoken on behalf of striking sanitation workers. Baldwin was in Palm Springs, California, working on the Malcolm X screenplay when he heard about King's murder; a friend's telephone call had delivered the awful news.

Baldwin stopped his work and traveled to Atlanta for King's funeral on April 7 in the Ebenezer Baptist Church, where King and his father had served as ministers. The small church was packed, and the streets leading to it were lined with mourners. Baldwin sat in a pew behind the actors Marlon Brando and Sidney Poitier and the entertainer Sammy Davis Jr. Baldwin later wrote that he tried not to weep during the funeral service because "tears seemed futile."[61] On the way out of the church after the service, however, walking between Sammy Davis Jr. and Marlon Brando, Baldwin broke down. "I started to cry," he later wrote, "and I stumbled, and Sammy grabbed my arm. We started to walk."[62]

Writing Projects

During these tumultuous years, Baldwin still found time to write. In fact, the events of the Civil Rights movement inspired perhaps his greatest period of productivity. Between 1960 and 1968, he published two novels and a collection of short stories, brought a play to Broadway, and published dozens of essays, some of which are among his best. The great civil rights events in which he took part seemed to spur his literary imagination.

Although Baldwin's novels cover a wide variety of subjects, he returns to certain themes again and again. His fictional characters are often artists adrift in an unstable world. For example, Rufus Scott, one of the main characters in his third novel, *Another Country*, published in 1962, is a black jazz drummer, trying to hold on to a romantic relationship with Leona, a white woman from the South, despite the racial tensions that arise between them. The relationship deteriorates, and Leona suffers a serious psychological breakdown. When Leona returns to the South with her mother, Rufus commits suicide by jumping off the George Washington Bridge. In his review of *Another Country*, Granville Hicks called the book "one of the most powerful novels of our time."[63]

Tell Me How Long the Train's Been Gone, which appeared in 1968, features an African American actor, Leo Proudhammer, who despite a successful career finds himself lost. He has worked hard to escape the trap of the Harlem ghetto, but in doing so he has alienated himself from his fellow African Americans. Nonetheless, he does not quite fit in white society either. He has both female and male lovers, and this shifting sexual identity further confuses him.

Like Baldwin's first novel, *Go Tell It on the Mountain, Tell Me How Long the Train's Been Gone* is loosely autobiographical. Like Proudhammer, Baldwin is an artist who has escaped the Harlem ghetto and who had,

Saying Good-Bye to Martin Luther King Jr.

Baldwin describes King's funeral in No Name in the Street, *an autobiography published in 1972.*

"The actual service sort of washed over me, in waves. It wasn't that it seemed unreal; it was the most real church service I've ever sat through in my life, or ever hope to sit through; but I have a childhood hangover thing about not weeping in public, and I was concentrating on holding myself together. I did not weep for Martin; tears seemed futile. But I may also have been afraid, and I could not have been the only one, that if I began to weep, I would not be able to stop. There was more than enough to weep for, if one was to weep—so many of us, cut down, so soon. Medgar, Malcolm, Martin; and their widows, and their children."

at least for a time during his years in Paris, separated himself from his fellow African Americans. Baldwin and Proudhammer were both bisexual as well. The strategy of using personal issues and concerns to shape his fictional characters is one that Baldwin used frequently to good effect.

Eloquent Essays

But Baldwin is often at his best in the essay rather than in fiction. The essays published during this period eloquently articulate the racial problems facing America—the lack of spirit in the urban ghettos, the inhumanity of segregation, the need in America for a radical change in race relations. Yet these essays offer an honest hope that racial tensions will ease. For example, in "My Dungeon Shook," a public letter addressed to his nephew, included in *The Fire Next Time*, Baldwin states:

> And if the word *integration* means anything, this is what it means: that we, with love, shall force our brothers to see themselves as they are, to cease fleeing from reality and begin to change it. For this is your home, my friend, do not be driven from it; great men have done great things here, and will again, and we can make America what America must become.[64]

The passage, written in 1962, before the deaths of Evers and King, suggests the sense of optimism that Baldwin gained as the Civil Rights movement moved forward. Baldwin, the man who fled America for another country, advises his nephew not to turn his back on his homeland. He asserts that the United States might someday become the great country that King later envisioned in his "I Have a Dream" speech. Baldwin concludes *The Fire Next Time* with the hope that "we may be able, handful that we are, to end the racial nightmare, and achieve our country, and change the history of the world."[65]

After King's death, Baldwin's work would be somewhat less hopeful, and he would involve himself less directly in political affairs; but he continued to write and explore important social issues.

6 Bitter Years

The death of Martin Luther King Jr. had a profound effect on James Baldwin. Baldwin had always hoped that America could solve its racial problems and achieve the just society that King had called for. After King's assassination, however, Baldwin became cynical and bitter. "I think there was a change in him over the years," said Kenneth Clark, a psychologist and educator active in the Civil Rights movement who knew Baldwin well. "I had a feeling as time went on Jim became less and less hopeful about positive changes in America as far as race is concerned."[66] The actor Billy Dee Williams, a close friend, made the same point. "Martin Luther King's death was with Jimmy a long time," Williams told one Baldwin biographer. "I doubt he ever got over it. . . . Much of his hope died with King."[67]

In an interview a year or so after King's death, Baldwin himself put into

Martin Luther King's death affected Baldwin so intensely that the writer lost hope in America ever being able to solve its race problems.

A Changed Man

W. J. Weatherby, one of James Baldwin's biographers, describes how Baldwin changed in the years after Martin Luther King's death.

"The change I noticed over the years was a gradual aging—more rapid after King's death and the decline of the civil rights movement—and the fieriness within him that could light up his eyes and set his finger wagging slowly growing less intense until he became almost mellow, the old fire still there but smoldering now. The boyish idealism, the belief in integration, the optimism about the future—all this changed into a kind of disillusionment, almost resignation. . . .

He celebrated his fiftieth birthday the same year—1974—that *Beale Street* was published, and with far less emotion than he had shown on his fortieth. He seemed to have a series of illnesses as if, having overspent his energy, he had become a temporary burnt-out case. Yet having at last established a settled home, he seemed unable to stay there for long before, restless again, he was off to the airport."

words the pessimism that he felt in the wake of King's assassination.

> Well, we've marched and petitioned for a decade, and now it's clear that there's no point in marching or petitioning. . . . And what happens I don't know, but when they killed Martin they killed that hope.[68]

Not only was Baldwin less optimistic after King's death; he was also fearful for his own life. Medgar Evers, Malcolm X, Martin Luther King Jr.—all were Baldwin's comrades in the civil rights struggle, and all had been murdered. Baldwin thought that he might be next, and he decided within a year after King's death to return to Europe for a time. He would spend much of the next several years living in France and Istanbul, a Turkish city that Baldwin had first visited in the early 1960s and that would become, as Baldwin biographer W. J. Weatherby put it, "a new refuge that he would return to many times over the next ten years."[69] Shortly after returning to Paris, Baldwin explained his reasons for again leaving his homeland:

> I suppose my decision was made when Malcolm X was killed, when Martin Luther King was killed, when Medgar Evers [was killed]. I loved Medgar. I loved Martin and Malcolm. We all worked together and kept the faith together. Now they were all dead. When you think about it, it is incredible. I'm

the last witness—everybody else is dead. I couldn't stay in America, I had to leave.[70]

For about two years after King's death, Baldwin suffered a terrible case of writer's block; he even had trouble sitting down to write a letter. Late in his life, Baldwin recalled that time: "I didn't think I could write at all. I didn't see any point to it. I was hurt. . . . I can't even talk about it. I didn't know how to continue, didn't see my way clear."[71]

Talking About Race

Even though Baldwin had trouble writing for a time after King's death, he did not remain completely silent on racial issues. He articulated his views in a number of interviews with editors, reporters, and talk-show hosts. By this time he and his books were well known, both in the United States and abroad, and his frank statements on America's racial tensions were often reported in the news, sometimes making the headlines.

One of Baldwin's most noteworthy and controversial interviews was with television talk-show host David Frost a year after King's death. When Frost suggested that many white Americans had changed their views of black people for the better because of the Civil Rights movement, Baldwin was quick to point out that many had not. "We're on the edge of a civil war,"[72] Baldwin told Frost. Later in the conversation, Baldwin made his point more clearly:

Something very important is happening in this country now, and I think for the first time the people legally white and the people legally black are

Letter to a Prisoner

A letter published in The New York Review of Books *in 1971 reveals the bitterness James Baldwin felt in the years after Martin Luther King's death.*

"We know that we, the blacks, and not only we, the blacks, have been, and are, the victims of a system whose only fuel is greed, whose only god is profit. We know that the fruits of this system have been ignorance, despair, and death, and we know that the system is doomed because the world can no longer afford it—if, indeed, it ever could have. And we know that, for the perpetuation of this system, we have all been mercilessly brutalized, and have been told nothing but lies, lies about ourselves and our kinsmen and our past, and about love, life, and death, so that both soul and body have been bound in hell."

beginning to understand that if they do not come together they're going to end up in the same gas oven.[73]

Frost assumed that Baldwin was comparing the plight of black people in America to the plight of Jews held captive in Nazi concentration camps during World War II. Millions of Jews taken to the camps had been gassed to death in huge ovenlike chambers.

Frost thought that such a comparison was far-fetched. "Gas oven?" Frost asked. "That's overstating the point, isn't it?" "So were the Jews in Germany told that," Baldwin replied. Frost again sought clarification: "But there's no parallel, surely." Baldwin's response was quick and sharp: "There is a parallel, if you were born in Harlem." Frost pointed out that the United States never had a policy for mass extermination for African Americans like the one implemented by Germany to eliminate the Jews before and during World War II. But Baldwin pressed the issue.

> I will tell you this, my friend, for every Sammy Davis, for every Jimmy Baldwin, for every black cat you have heard of in the history of this country, there are a hundred of us dead. . . . I can carry you to some of the graveyards, where boys just like me, or brighter than me, more beautiful than me, perished because they were black.[74]

A Bitter Time

Baldwin's comments illustrate the bitterness and pessimism he felt in the wake of King's death. That bitterness also surfaced in a recorded discussion that he had with

In a talk with anthropologist Margaret Mead (above), Baldwin discussed his frustration with the slow progress of the Civil Rights movement after King's death.

Margaret Mead, the anthropologist, in August 1970. The conversation, initiated by Mead and lasting several hours, covered many political and personal topics. (It was later published in book form under the title *A Rap on Race*.) Baldwin's comments reflect the anger that he felt as the Civil Rights movement seemed to lose its energy after King's death. For example, when Mead brought up the tragic race riots that had taken place in Newark, Detroit, and other American cities in recent years, Baldwin responded: "To be in the ghetto is to be a kind of prisoner, more or less official, of the state. And if nothing belongs to you, there is no reason not to burn it down, especially if it is oppressive."[75]

Several times during this conversation, Mead asked about Baldwin's decision to leave America again and live in Europe. "My country drove me out," Baldwin

A news photograph captures a heated moment during a race riot in Newark. Baldwin tried to explain the desperation that led to riots in Newark and other cities.

explained when Mead brought up that issue. "The Americans drove me out of my country."[76] His first departure in 1948 had been a matter of choice; now he was claiming that he was actually forced out of his homeland. Baldwin again made clear how profoundly King's death affected him:

> There was a time in my life not so very long ago that I believed, hoped . . . that this country could become what it has always presented as what it wanted to become. But I am sorry, no matter how this may sound: When Martin was murdered for me that hope ended.[77]

Writing About Race

Eventually, Baldwin did begin to write again. In 1970 he purchased an estate of several acres in the town of Saint Paul-de-Vence in southern France, and he found

this setting very conducive for writing. His next two books reflect the bitterness that surfaced during the Frost and Mead interviews.

In 1972 Baldwin published *No Name in the Street*, a book-length autobiography that focused on his activities during the Civil Rights movement. The book is more bitter, less hopeful than earlier autobiographical pieces like the essay "Notes of a Native Son" and the book *The Fire Next Time*. In *No Name in the Street*, Baldwin advances his belief that the political leaders of white America are determined to destroy their countrymen of color:

> Black men have been burned alive in this country more than once—many men now living have seen it with their own eyes; black men and boys are being murdered here today, in cold blood, and with impunity; and it is a very serious matter when the govern-

ment which is sworn to protect the interests of all American citizens publicly and unabashedly allies itself with the enemies of black men.[78]

Baldwin also confesses his fear that the increasing tensions between whites and blacks might lead to a new wave of racial violence. Although he states that he has no desire "to see a generation perish in the streets," Baldwin asserts that Americans are "at present the most dishonorable and violent people in the world," and that they should not be surprised if violence destroys their society. "People who treat other people as less than human must not be surprised when the bread they have cast on the waters comes floating back to them, poisoned."[79]

Critics who reviewed *No Name in the Street* immediately noted its angrier, more hostile tone. Benjamin DeMott, reviewing the book in *Saturday Review*, understood this new voice. Though he preferred Baldwin's earlier autobiographical works, DeMott sensed the reasons for the new shrillness in Baldwin's writings. He noted that repeatedly during the previous decade "the author of *The Fire Next Time* has had to seek within himself both the energies and the vocabulary of fury—to search for the words that will make real the latest atrocity." DeMott believed that that effort took its toll on Baldwin, resulting in the harsh tone of this recent book:

> To function as a voice of outrage month after month for a decade and more strains heart and mind, and rhetoric as well; the consequence is a writing style ever on the edge of being winded by too many summonses to intensity.[80]

This same tone is evident in Baldwin's next novel, *If Beale Street Could Talk*, published in 1974. The novel bitterly attacks the American judicial system, which in

Baldwin outside the house he purchased in Saint Paul-de-Vence after moving back to southern France.

In this passage from A Rap on Race, James Baldwin comments on how black children's self-image is destroyed at an early age.

"By teaching a black child that he is worthless, that he can never contribute anything to civilization, you're teaching him how to hate his mother, his father, and his brothers. Everyone in my generation has seen the wreckage that this has caused. And what black kids are doing now, no matter how excessively, is right. They are refusing this entire frame of reference and they are saying to the Republic: This is your bill, this is your bloody bill written in my *blood*, and you are going to have to pay it."

Baldwin's view is determined to destroy young black people, especially those with intelligence and talent. Tish, the narrator, is a nineteen-year-old unmarried and pregnant black woman living in Harlem. The novel centers on a young black artist, Tish's fiancé Fonny, who has been jailed for a rape that he did not commit. Early in the novel Tish explains how the legal system preys on poor people, like her unjustly imprisoned fiancé:

> If you cross the Sahara, and you fall, by and by vultures circle around you, smelling, sensing your death. They circle lower and lower: they wait. They know. They know when the flesh is ready, when the spirit cannot fight back. The poor are always crossing the Sahara. And the lawyers and bondsmen and all that crowd circle around the poor, exactly like vultures.[81]

Despite this bleak picture, Tish is sustained by her family's support and Fonny's love. As the novel ends Fonny is still in prison awaiting his trial, but Tish imagines a day when she is caring for her baby and Fonny is sculpting in his studio—a note of hope in an otherwise pessimistic novel.

If Beale Street Could Talk received mixed reviews. The reviewer for the *New York Times*, Anatole Broyard, reacted to the novel's bitterness and condemned it as an attack on white people. Some reviewers found it wanting in comparison to earlier Baldwin novels, and a few critics suggested that its author, now fifty years old, was losing some of his literary powers. But other reviewers were more sympathetic, and the book stayed on the best-seller lists for several weeks.

Whether Baldwin's literary powers declined in the years after King's death is a matter for literary critics and historians to debate. But certainly the tone of both his spoken comments and his writings had changed. The tumultuous events of the 1960s had a profound effect on James Baldwin. They had aged him and disillusioned him. He found some solace in Istanbul and in Saint Paul-de-Vence, but not a lasting peace.

7 Final Words

The last decade of James Baldwin's life was not artistically satisfying. He started several projects that he never completed—a book on Martin Luther King Jr., Malcolm X, and Medgar Evers; several screenplays; a novel based on his long-time friend, the artist Beauford Delaney. Poor health and bouts of depression brought on by his health stymied his productivity.

Final Projects

Reviewers and the reading public did not receive Baldwin's final books as enthusiastically as they had his earlier ones. *The Devil Finds Work*, an extended essay on the roles that blacks played in American movies, was published in 1976 to mixed reviews. His last novel, *Just Above My Head*, published three years later, experienced a similar critical reception.

This final Baldwin novel, his longest, took about five years to complete. It is the story of Arthur Montana, a black singer who has died in the men's room of a London pub. The narrator is Arthur's brother, Hall, and his meandering narrative recounts Arthur's life of pain and dissipation from the streets of Harlem to the barrooms of London. Like so many other

Baldwin's final novel, Just Above My Head, *received mixed reviews upon its publication in 1979. The novel's principal character, Arthur Montana, shares many characteristics with Baldwin.*

Baldwin characters, Arthur is a mirror of Baldwin himself: the anguished artist, an African American and a homosexual, searching for peace in a world that makes him feel like an outsider. Reviewers recognized Baldwin's ambition in crafting this long, complex story, but the reviews were lukewarm at best.

In the spring of 1981, Baldwin embarked on a project that would lead to his last original nonfiction book. *Playboy* magazine commissioned him to travel to Atlanta to write an article on a series of murders of young black children that had recently occurred in that city. Rather than doing a focused reporter's investigation of the murders, Baldwin used the case as background to address a larger issue—the position of blacks in the "new" South, the South that had supposedly changed as a result of the Civil Rights movement. Baldwin found that Atlanta, at least, had not substantially changed, even though the city's first black mayor, Andrew Young, was one of King's lieutenants. Baldwin saw the murdered black children as evidence that African Americans were still detested in that southern city. That the prime suspect in the case (the man eventually convicted) was black did not alter Baldwin's conclusions.

Baldwin completed the article, which won a prize as *Playboy*'s best nonfiction article in 1981, and expanded it to book form under the title *The Evidence of Things Not Seen*. Baldwin's editors at Dial Press, however, found the work unsatisfactory and decided not to publish it, so Baldwin sold the book to Holt, Rinehart, and Winston, another publisher. The book did not receive the attention that early Baldwin books had received. A new Baldwin book would often be reviewed on the front page of the *New York Times Book Review*, but *The Evidence of Things Not Seen* received only a short review near the end of the section.

Baldwin was upset that he had difficulty finding a publisher for *The Evidence of Things Not Seen*, and he was also dismayed by the lack of critical attention and poor reviews that the book received. Baldwin surmised that there might be a con-

James Baldwin was greatly dismayed when his book, The Evidence of Things Not Seen, *received poor reviews. In his bitterness, Baldwin concluded that publishers and reviewers had conspired to silence his controversial work.*

spiracy among publishers and reviewers to silence his pen. No evidence existed for such a charge. Joseph Campbell, a friend and later biographer of Baldwin, asserts that *The Evidence of Things Not Seen* was, quite simply, a poorly written book. According to Campbell, Baldwin did not add anything of substance by expanding the work from a six-thousand-word article to a sixty-thousand-word book. "The book was padded out with anecdotes about his childhood, and polemics directed against the 'Republic.'"[82] Campbell also notes that Baldwin had not done sufficient research for the book; Baldwin's belief that Wayne Williams, the man eventually convicted of the murders, was innocent was based on a hunch rather than on evidence.

Baldwin's final book, *The Price of the Ticket*, was a collection of his nonfiction writings from 1948 through 1985. All of the essays contained in the collection had appeared earlier in magazines and journals, and some had appeared in his earlier essay collections, *Notes of a Native Son* and *Nobody Knows My Name*. Baldwin was very satisfied with the new book, which (he felt) collected all his best essays in one volume. But the magazine and newspaper reviewers paid little attention to the collection, perhaps because its contents had already appeared in print.

Disappointment and Renewal

Baldwin was disheartened by the mediocre reviews that greeted his final books. He believed that he had lost none of his literary powers and that the literary critics and reviewers were ignoring or condemning him because they were offended by his continued attention to racial issues. Critics and biographers looking back on Baldwin's career today, however, generally concur that like many other great writers—the novelists Ernest Hemingway and William Faulkner, the playwrights Arthur Miller and Tennessee Williams—Baldwin did his best work before his fiftieth birthday.

But Baldwin was pleased with several awards that he received in the final decade of his life. He received honorary degrees from Morehouse College in Atlanta in 1976, the University of Massachusetts in 1978, and City University of New York in 1982. In 1986 he was presented the prestigious French Legion of Honor by President François Mitterand. This award is bestowed upon individuals who have brought honor to the Republic of France.

Another highlight for Baldwin during those years was the telecast of a film version of *Go Tell It on the Mountain* on Public Broadcasting System's *American Playhouse* series. The film, which starred Paul Winfield as John Grimes, greatly pleased Baldwin, who felt that the screenplay had vividly brought his novel to life. He hoped that more of his fictional works might be brought to the screen, but none others appeared during his lifetime.

Professor Baldwin

During his final years Baldwin also found great pleasure in teaching. In the spring of 1978, Bowling Green State University, in Ohio, invited Baldwin to serve as a special guest lecturer, and he taught courses there in American literature and creative writing. Energized by the young people

(Left) Baldwin and symphony conductor Leonard Bernstein pose for a photo after both received the prestigious French Legion of Honor, an award given to those who bring honor to France. (Below) Baldwin talks with a student at Bowling Green State University, where he served as a visiting professor for several semesters.

whom he taught, Baldwin twice returned to Bowling Green, for the fall semester of 1979 and again in the fall of 1981.

In September of 1983, Baldwin accepted a position as visiting professor for Five Colleges Inc. in Massachusetts. His position required that he teach courses at five colleges in the Amherst area—the University of Massachusetts, Hampshire College, Mount Holyoke College, Smith College, and Amherst College. He continued at this post for three years, and he enjoyed the experience, though he sometimes had difficulty adjusting to this rigid academic schedule. He engaged students in lively debate; he encouraged young writers; and he befriended students and faculty members, often inviting them home for lunch and dinner.

At Amherst College, Baldwin befriended an Afro-American Studies Department professor, John Edgar Wideman, the African American novelist. And Baldwin became a big hit at faculty parties. With a drink in his hand he would explain his views on racial and literary matters to his fascinated colleagues. But what he enjoyed most was working with students. He referred to them as "the children"; it was one of the few opportunities that the childless Baldwin had to work with young people, and the work delighted him.

Poor health, however, curtailed Baldwin's teaching career. Teaching, traveling back and forth from France to the United States, and writing took a toll on Baldwin during his final years. During the summer of 1983, he suffered a mild heart attack. Throughout his life Baldwin had had poor health habits. He chain-smoked, sometimes drank excessively, and had a poor diet. After his sixtieth birthday, his health began to deteriorate rapidly.

Final Days

Early in 1987, back in France, Baldwin began to complain to friends about a sore throat that would not go away. His deep baritone voice grew hoarse and swallowing became difficult. At first he avoided treat-

Baldwin loved teaching. He took great pleasure in engaging his students in lively debate and offered encouragement to young, aspiring writers.

ment, hoping that the problem was merely a long-lingering winter cold that would resolve itself. Finally, in early April he consulted a doctor, who diagnosed his problem as cancer of the esophagus.

Baldwin underwent surgery on April 25 in a hospital near Nice in southern France. Part of his esophagus was removed, but the cancer had already spread to Baldwin's liver. The prognosis was not good, but Baldwin convalesced at his home in Saint Paul-de-Vence with his brother David and other good friends in residence to assist him.

Baldwin regained some of his strength during the warm summer months; he continued to write, but he would not live much longer. The cancer had spread throughout his body. During the fall of 1987 his condition worsened, and he was confined to his bed for much of the day. By Thanksgiving Baldwin was so weak that he could barely eat the dinner that friends had cooked for him.

Baldwin died in bed with his friends at his side on the evening of December 1. In his final moments, his brother David kissed him and said, "It's all right, Jimmy; you can cross over now."[83] His friend Bernard Hassell said that Baldwin "had a quiet and painless death . . . with great dignity."[84]

Reaction of Sadness and Appreciation

The literary world reacted with sadness and appreciation when Baldwin's death was announced. Ralph Ellison, the African American novelist who authored *Invisible Man*, called Baldwin one of America's "most gifted writers, one of the most important American essayists, black or white." Henry Louis Gates, a scholar of African American literature, said that Baldwin's death was

> a great loss not only for black people, but to the country as a whole, for which he served as a conscience [and that Baldwin] educated an entire generation of Americans about the civil rights struggle and the sensibility of Afro-Americans as we faced and conquered the final barriers in our long quest for civil rights.

Benjamin DeMott, a reviewer of Baldwin's books and a professor at Amherst College, echoed Gates and Ellison. "I would place him very high among writers," he said, "in part because his work showed a powerful commitment to the right values and had a profound impact for good on our culture."[85]

The day after Baldwin died, his body was laid out for the people of Saint Paul-de-Vence to pay their respects. Then the body was shipped to New York for a funeral service and burial. The wake was held in a Harlem funeral home in the neighborhood where he had grown up, and the funeral service took place at the Cathedral of St. John the Divine, a grand Gothic-style cathedral in New York City.

Baldwin's funeral was the first to be held in the Cathedral of St. John the Divine since the funeral of Duke Ellington, the great bandleader and composer, who died in 1974. The large church was filled with Baldwin's family members, including his elderly mother, Emma Berdis Baldwin, friends, reporters, writers, and politicians. Baldwin's nephew Trevor sang psalms, and his sister Gloria's sister-in-law, the

Paying Respects

In his book Stealing the Fire: The Art and Protest of James Baldwin, *Horace A. Porter describes the mourners at James Baldwin's funeral at the Cathedral of St. John the Divine. Baldwin had touched the lives of many different types of people.*

"The front of the cathedral had been reserved for the family, friends, and honored guests. Cathedral officials and workers arranged flowers, lit candles, and went purposefully about their business. Reporters started rushing in. They focused and clicked their cameras, taking shots of the coffin bearing Baldwin's body, draped in black at the front of the cathedral. The crowd thickened now. . . . There were women in business suits, women with their heads wrapped in turbans, women with braided hair, glamorous black women in full-length fur coats. There were distinguished gentlemen, and other men not so well-heeled. One young black man wore a New York Yankees baseball cap, with a profusion of braids sprouting out the back."

During a funeral service at the Cathedral of St. John the Divine in New York, friends, family, and admirers mourn the loss of the man and the writer.

A Tribute from the *New York Times*

The day after James Baldwin's death, the New York Times *paid tribute to one of New York's greatest writers. An excerpt from the editorial follows.*

"Few writers so define a movement or moment as did James Baldwin, who died yesterday at the age of 63. In the 1950's and 1960's, his searing essays on racial discrimination in the United States gave passionate voice to the emerging civil rights movement.

. . . His angry words embodied the struggle of blacks, in the North and South, who defied laws and customs that barred them from motels, pushed them to the backs of buses, denied them jobs and service at lunch counters, refused them the right to vote and even to hope.

Mr. Baldwin saw himself not as a provocateur but as a 'witness.' He felt it was the role of the writer to define the society he observes. Yet his passionate writing roused Americans black and white to attack the terrible legacy of racism. His voice was, and is, a powerful weapon in that struggle."

The New York Times *marked James Baldwin's passing with an editorial praising his "passionate writing" and his powerful voice in the struggle to end racism in America.*

Reverend Rena Karefa-Smart, read from the Scriptures. The pop singer Odetta led the congregation in the singing of hymns and traditional African American spirituals, and the writers Maya Angelou and Toni Morrison spoke eloquently of Baldwin's life and art. The main eulogy was delivered by Amiri Baraka, the African American poet whom Baldwin had met and befriended during the civil rights battles of the 1960s. Near the end of the funeral service, a recording of Baldwin singing the hymn "Precious Lord" was played.

Baldwin was buried in Ferncliff Cemetery in Harstdale, New York, a suburb of New York City. His grave was set near those of Paul Robeson, the great African American singer and actor, and Malcolm X. James Baldwin would rest in good company.

8 James Baldwin's Legacy

James Baldwin is best remembered as an eloquent writer. He was a talented novelist who confronted issues that many Americans ignored. He wrote plays that continue to move and thrill audiences. And he produced a body of essays that rank him among great American essayists like Ralph Waldo Emerson, Henry David Thoreau, and Frederick Douglass.

But James Baldwin's importance extends beyond the thousands of pages of splendid prose that he produced. Besides being a writer, he was a social and political activist, a role model for young people everywhere, and a mentor for aspiring writers.

Baldwin the Activist

Baldwin sometimes tried to downplay his role as an activist or spokesman for the African American cause. He did not think of himself as a political leader. He once said that his main contribution to the Civil Rights movement was his ability to get a story past an editor's desk. In other words,

Baldwin, pictured with a boy admitted to an integrated school, held a keen interest in America's youth and served as a role model for many young people.

he believed that he promoted civil rights mainly by confronting racial issues in his novels, essays, and plays.

Baldwin was surely an activist with his pen and typewriter, but he was too modest in denying his role as a spokesman and public speaker. In 1957 when the Civil Rights movement began gaining energy in the United States, Baldwin left the comfort of Paris and returned to his homeland to join the struggle. He traveled around the South and wrote truthfully about what he saw at a time when outspoken black men were often the victims of violence. He marched in the marches, and he spoke at the rallies, using his experi-

Through his role as writer, speaker, and political activist, Baldwin was able to address the racial difficulties in America and help bring these pressing issues to light.

ence as a self-trained preacher to move his audiences.

After the death of Martin Luther King Jr., Baldwin partially withdrew from the civil rights battles. Nonetheless, he continued to speak and write on America's troubled race relations until the day he died. In doing so, he helped awaken a complacent nation to the racial problems that it had ignored for so long.

Baldwin the Role Model

Baldwin was raised on the mean streets of Harlem, where drugs, violence, and alcohol took the lives of many. Yet he refused to be trapped by the dangerous and spiritless environment or defeated by the wreckage around him.

Young people today can learn a valuable lesson from James Baldwin. At a very young age, he set an almost unreachable goal: to become a great writer. With hard work, patience, and fortitude in the face of setbacks, he reached his goal—perhaps excelling even beyond the high standard that he had set for himself. And when Baldwin achieved success, when he became very famous and somewhat wealthy as a result of his books, he did not forget the place from which he came. He returned often to Harlem; more importantly his writing prompted all Americans, black and white, to confront the nation's racial problems.

Baldwin was wise enough to realize that not everyone could overcome a harsh environment as he himself had done. For every James Baldwin, he knew that hundreds of youngsters were defeated by the obstacles of the ghetto. But his life sug-

A Biographer's Tribute

David Leeming's 1994 book, James Baldwin: A Biography, *pays a fitting tribute to its subject.*

"Baldwin was a prophet not so much in the tradition of foreseeing events . . . as in the tradition of the Old Testament. Like Ezekiel, Isaiah, Jeremiah, and Samuel, whose words and agonies he knew from his days as a child preacher in Harlem, he understood that as a witness he must often stand alone in anger against a nation that seemed intent on not 'keeping the faith.'. . .

Baldwin's prophecy took many forms. His essays stand out as among the most articulate expressions we have of the human condition in his time. The collections *Notes of a Native Son* and *Nobody Knows My Name,* and the long essay *The Fire Next Time,* have already become classics. In three plays, many short stories, and six novels . . . Baldwin creates parables to illustrate, in the private and personal realm of human relationships, the words of his essays.

. . . In his personal life and his work, he took the side of those who were made into exiles and outcasts by barriers of race, sex, and class or who turned away from safety and chose the honorable path of tearing down such barriers. But he mourned for those who had created the barriers and had unwittingly allowed themselves to be destroyed by them."

gests that it is worthwhile for people, especially young people, to keep hope alive, even in the grimmest of circumstances.

Baldwin the Mentor

When Baldwin began to write professionally in the late 1940s, only a handful of African Americans made a living by writing. African American youngsters were much more likely to aspire to careers as athletes than as authors. Editors and publishing companies did not make great efforts to seek out talented black writers and bring their work to the public's attention.

Baldwin helped open the literary establishment's doors to African American authors. The success of his books prompted editors and publishers to consider the literary efforts of other African American writers. The black arts movement, an outpouring of literary and visual artistic works that commenced in the 1960s, was an extension of the literary successes of writers like Baldwin a decade earlier. Many of the talented African American writers who emerged from this movement—Ishmael Reed, Nikki Giovanni, Alice Walker—might not have found receptive editors and readers had Baldwin not helped prepare the way.

Appropriately, three of today's most eloquent African American writers spoke at Baldwin's funeral: the Nobel Prize–winning novelist Toni Morrison, the poet and playwright Amiri Baraka, and the poet and narrative writer Maya Angelou.

Morrison thanked Baldwin for three gifts that he had bestowed upon her. First, she thanked him for giving her "a language to dwell in." As she explained, "No one possessed or inhabited language for me in the way you did. You made American English honest—genuinely international." For Morrison, Baldwin had stripped American English of its hypocrisy; he had "replaced lumbering platitudes with an upright elegance." Next, she thanked him for his courage—a courage "to recognize and identify evil but never fear or stand in awe of it." Lastly, Morrison thanked Baldwin for a gift that surfaced in the presence of his closest friends—his gift of tenderness, "a tenderness, of vulnerability, that asked everything, expected everything and . . . provided us with the ways and means to deliver."[86]

Baraka made an equally eloquent tribute. He spoke of Baldwin as a friend and older brother:

As a man, he was my friend, my older brother he would joke, not really jok-

---

A Tribute from *Newsweek*

A week after Baldwin's death, Peter S. Prescott wrote an appraisal of James Baldwin's career for Newsweek *magazine. Here is the introduction from that essay.*

"Always he felt himself an exile: because he was black and ambivalent about his religion and his sexuality. Last week James Baldwin, 63, died of stomach cancer at his home in Saint Paul-de-Vence in southern France. For three decades he had served as our Jeremiah, raging against the abomination of American racism. He wrote novels, plays, stories and above all essays that combined polemic with autobiography. The last were not easily arrived at: a polemic requires a certain public distance, yet Baldwin's autobiographies were intensely personal. He yoked these two seemingly incompatible forms together, as no one in recent memory had, and the combination worked so well that for a time Baldwin seemed a more important writer than history will probably judge him to be."

James Baldwin's passion, eloquence, and generosity touched many lives.

cized, made beautiful, analyzed, cajoled, lyricized, attacked, sang, made us think, made us better, made us consciously human.[87]

Angelou (who would later read a poem at President Clinton's inauguration) credited Baldwin with energizing her literary career by encouraging her to write the story of her childhood, later published in 1969 as the celebrated autobiography, *I Know Why the Caged Bird Sings*. Like Baraka, Angelou came to see Baldwin as a brother, one who knew "that brother's love redeems a sister's pain."[88]

Had they had the opportunity, many of Baldwin's readers, less famous perhaps than the three writers who spoke at his funeral, could have made similar statements. His books sold hundreds of thousands of copies throughout his lifetime and reached and moved readers around the world. Baldwin did more than write and sell books; he changed lives.

To a new generation of readers, James Baldwin remains alive. His body was laid to rest in December of 1987, but his spirit lives in bookstores and on library shelves, or in any place that houses the literary works of this eloquent writer.

ing. As a man, he was Our friend. Our older or younger brother, we listened to him like we would somebody in our family. . . . [Baldwin] reported, criti-

Notes

Introduction: A Writer and Activist

1. James Baldwin, *Nobody Knows My Name*. New York: Vintage Books, 1993, p. 153.

Chapter 1: A Harlem Boyhood

2. James Baldwin, *Notes of a Native Son*. Boston: Beacon Press, 1983, p. 3.
3. Baldwin, *Nobody Knows My Name*, p. 57.
4. Baldwin, *Nobody Knows My Name*, p. 63.
5. Baldwin, *Notes of a Native Son*, p. 92.
6. James Baldwin, *No Name in the Street*. New York: Dell, 1972, p. 5.
7. Baldwin, *No Name in the Street*, p. 5.
8. "Conversation: Ida Lewis and James Baldwin," in Fred L. Standley and Louis H. Pratt, eds., *Conversations with James Baldwin*. Jackson: University Press of Mississippi, 1989, p. 89.
9. James Baldwin, *The Fire Next Time*. New York: Vintage Books, 1993, p. 19.
10. Baldwin, *The Fire Next Time*, p. 19.
11. Baldwin, *The Fire Next Time*, p. 20.
12. Baldwin, *The Fire Next Time*, p. 19.
13. Baldwin, *The Fire Next Time*, p. 20.
14. Baldwin, *The Fire Next Time*, pp. 29–30.
15. Baldwin, *The Fire Next Time*, p. 33.
16. Baldwin, *The Fire Next Time*, p. 34.
17. Quoted in James Campbell, *Talking at the Gates: A Life of James Baldwin*. New York: Viking, 1991, p. 16.
18. Quoted in Campbell, *Talking at the Gates*, p. 18.
19. Baldwin, *Notes of a Native Son*, p. 108.

Chapter 2: Leaving Home

20. Baldwin, *Notes of a Native Son*, p. 93.
21. Baldwin, *Notes of a Native Son*, p. 94.
22. Baldwin, *Notes of a Native Son*, p. 86.
23. Baldwin, *Notes of a Native Son*, p. 107.
24. Baldwin, *Notes of a Native Son*, p. 113.
25. Baldwin, *Notes of a Native Son*, p. 86.
26. "The Art of Fiction LXXVIII: James Baldwin," in Standley, *Conversations with James Baldwin*, p. 247.
27. David Leeming, *James Baldwin: A Biography*. New York: Knopf, 1994, p. 51.
28. Baldwin, *Notes of a Native Son*, pp. 67–69.
29. Baldwin, *Notes of a Native Son*, pp. 71–72.
30. Quoted in Campbell, *Talking at the Gates*, p. 41.

Chapter 3: A Writer in Paris

31. "The Art of Fiction LXXVIII: James Baldwin," in Standley, *Conversations with James Baldwin*, p. 233.
32. Leeming, *James Baldwin: A Biography*, p. 56.
33. Baldwin, *Notes of a Native Son*, p. 14.
34. Baldwin, *Notes of a Native Son*, p. 23.
35. Quoted in W. J. Weatherby, *James Baldwin: Artist on Fire*. New York: Donald I. Fine, 1989, p. 75.
36. Baldwin, *Notes of a Native Son*, p. 158.
37. Baldwin, *Nobody Knows My Name*, p. 5.
38. James Baldwin, *Go Tell It on the Mountain*. New York: Dial Press, 1963, p. 43.
39. Baldwin, *Go Tell It on the Mountain*, pp. 234–35.

40. Donald Barr, "Guilt Was Everywhere," *New York Times Book Review*, May 17, 1953, p. 27.

41. Langston Hughes, "From Harlem to Paris," *New York Times Book Review*, February 26, 1956, p. 26.

42. Quoted in Leeming, *James Baldwin: A Biography*, p. 118.

Chapter 4: An Exile's Return

43. Quoted in Daniel J. Boorstin, ed., *An American Primer*. New York: Meridian, 1985, p. 93.

44. Baldwin, *No Name in the Street*, p. 50.

45. Baldwin, *No Name in the Street*, p. 71.

46. Baldwin, *No Name in the Street*, p. 68.

47. Baldwin, *Nobody Knows My Name*, p. 104.

48. Baldwin, *Nobody Knows My Name*, p. 104.

49. James Baldwin, "The High Road to Destiny," in C. Eric Lincoln, ed., *Martin Luther King, Jr.: A Profile*. New York: Hill and Wang, 1970, p. 90.

50. Baldwin, "The High Road to Destiny," p. 95.

51. Baldwin, *No Name in the Street*, p. 72.

52. Baldwin, *No Name in the Street*, p. 66.

53. Baldwin, *No Name in the Street*, p. 66.

54. Baldwin, *No Name in the Street*, p. 67.

55. Campbell, *Talking at the Gates*, pp. 124–25.

Chapter 5: The Writer as Political Activist

56. "The Art of Fiction LXXVIII: James Baldwin" in Standley, *Conversations with James Baldwin*, p. 241.

57. Martin Luther King Jr., "I Have a Dream," in James M. Washington, ed., *I Have a Dream: Writings and Speeches That Changed the World*. San Francisco: HarperSan Francisco, 1992, p. 104.

58. Baldwin, *No Name in the Street*, p. 140.

59. Baldwin, *No Name in the Street*, p. 153.

60. King, "Eulogy for the Martyred Children," in Washington, *I Have a Dream: Writings and Speeches That Changed the World*, p. 116.

61. Baldwin, *No Name in the Street*, p. 156.

62. Baldwin, *No Name in the Street*, p. 157.

63. Granville Hicks, "Outcasts in a Caldron of Hate," Fred L. Standley and Nancy V. Burt, eds., in *Critical Essays on James Baldwin*. Boston: G. K. Hall, 1988, p. 149.

64. Baldwin, *The Fire Next Time*, pp. 9–10.

65. Baldwin, *The Fire Next Time*, p. 105.

Chapter 6: Bitter Years

66. Quoted in Weatherby, *James Baldwin: Artist on Fire*, p. 299.

67. Quoted in Weatherby, *James Baldwin: Artist on Fire*, p. 297.

68. "James Baldwin Interviewed" in Standley, *Conversations with James Baldwin*, pp. 102–103.

69. Weatherby, *James Baldwin: Artist on Fire*, p. 177.

70. "Conversation: Ida Lewis and James Baldwin," in Standley, *Conversations with James Baldwin*. p. 85.

71. Quoted in Weatherby, *James Baldwin: Artist on Fire*, p. 300.

72. "Are We on the Edge of Civil War?" in Standley, *Conversations with James Baldwin*, p. 95.

73. "Are We on the Edge of Civil War?" in Standley, *Conversations with James Baldwin*, p. 96.

74. "Are We on the Edge of Civil War?" in Standley, *Conversations with James Baldwin*, pp. 96–97.

75. Margaret Mead and James Baldwin, *A Rap on Race*. Philadelphia: J. B. Lippincott, 1971, p. 141.

76. Mead and Baldwin, *A Rap on Race*, p. 221.

77. Mead and Baldwin, *A Rap on Race*, p. 244.

78. Baldwin, *No Name in the Street*, pp. 130–31.

79. Baldwin, *No Name in the Street*, pp. 191–92.

80. Benjamin DeMott, "James Baldwin on the Sixties: Acts and Revelations," in Kenneth Kinnamon, ed., *James Baldwin: A Collection of Critical Essays*. Englewood Cliffs, NJ: Prentice-Hall, 1974, p. 156.

81. James Baldwin, *If Beale Street Could Talk*. New York: Dell, 1974, p. 7.

Chapter 7: Final Words

82. Campbell, *Talking at the Gates*, pp. 266–67.

83. Quoted in Leeming, *James Baldwin: A Biography*, p. 386.

84. Quoted in Weatherby, *James Baldwin: Artist on Fire*, p. 372.

85. Lee A. Daniels, "James Baldwin, Eloquent Writer in Behalf of Civil Rights, Is Dead," *New York Times*, December 2, 1987, p. D-27.

Chapter 8: James Baldwin's Legacy

86. Toni Morrison, "Life in His Language," in "James Baldwin: His Voice Remembered," *New York Times Book Review*, December 20, 1987, p. 27.

87. Amiri Baraka, "We Carry Him as Us," in "James Baldwin: His Voice Remembered," p. 27.

88. Maya Angelou, "A Brother's Love," in "James Baldwin: His Voice Remembered," p. 29.

For Further Reading

Books About Baldwin

James Campbell, *Talking at the Gates: A Life of James Baldwin*. New York: Viking, 1991. The best book-length biography of Baldwin for junior high and high school students. It provides details of Baldwin's life and an overview of his literary works.

Fred L. Standley and Louis H. Pratt, eds., *Conversations with James Baldwin*. Jackson: University Press of Mississippi, 1989. Contains more than two dozen interviews with Baldwin, which include frank comments on his life, times, and literary works.

Books by Baldwin

Blues for Mister Charlie. New York: Dell, 1964. Baldwin's first produced play, set in the South during the Civil Rights movement.

The Fire Next Time. New York: Vintage Books, 1993. Contains the long autobiographical essay, "Letter from a Region in My Mind," that recounts episodes from Baldwin's childhood and young adulthood in Harlem.

Going to Meet the Man. New York: Dell, 1988. This collection contains eight short stories, most of which are appropriate for young readers.

Go Tell It on the Mountain. New York: Dial Press, 1963. Baldwin's first novel, recapturing his boyhood years in Harlem.

If Beale Street Could Talk. New York: Dell, 1974. Of Baldwin's novels this one, set in Harlem, is the most suitable for younger readers. It concerns a young woman's attempt to free her imprisoned fiancé, who has been falsely accused of a crime.

Nobody Knows My Name. New York: Vintage Books, 1993. Contains thirteen essays written between 1955 and 1961. The subjects include Baldwin's reflections on Harlem and his analysis of the Civil Rights movement.

No Name in the Street. New York: Dell, 1972. This book-length autobiography recounts Baldwin's experiences during the Civil Rights movement.

Notes of a Native Son. Boston: Beacon Press, 1983. Contains ten essays written between 1948 and 1955. The essays range in subject matter from Baldwin's boyhood years in Harlem to his expatriate life in Paris.

Works Consulted

James Baldwin, "An Open Letter to My Sister, Miss Angela Davis," *New York Review of Books,* January 17, 1971. A letter from Baldwin to a leader of the militant Black Panther Party.

———, *Another Country.* New York: Dial Press, 1962. Baldwin's third novel.

———, *The Price of the Ticket: Collected Non-Fiction, 1948–1985.* New York: St. Martin's/Marek, 1985. This volume includes most of the nonfiction that Baldwin wrote during his forty-year career.

Donald Barr, "Guilt Was Everywhere," *New York Times Book Review,* May 17, 1953. A review of Baldwin's first novel, *Go Tell It on the Mountain.*

Daniel J. Boorstin, ed., *An American Primer.* New York: Meridian, 1985. A collection of important American historical documents.

Taylor Branch, *Parting the Waters: America in the King Years, 1954–1963.* New York: Simon & Schuster, 1988. A detailed history of the first decade of the Civil Rights movement.

Lee A. Daniels, "James Baldwin, Eloquent Writer in Behalf of Civil Rights, Is Dead," *New York Times,* December 2, 1987. This obituary capsulizes Baldwin's life and summarizes reactions to his death.

Fern Marja Eckman, *The Furious Passage of James Baldwin.* New York: M. Evans, 1966. An early biography of Baldwin.

Langston Hughes, "From Harlem to Paris," *New York Times Book Review,* February 26, 1956. A review of *Notes of a Native Son.*

"James Baldwin's Fire," *New York Times,* December 2, 1987. An editorial that appeared in the *New York Times* after Baldwin's death.

"James Baldwin: His Voice Remembered," *New York Times Book Review,* December 20, 1987. This article contains eulogies read at Baldwin's funeral by Toni Morrison, Amiri Baraka, Maya Angelou, and William Styron.

Kenneth Kinnamon, ed., *James Baldwin: A Collection of Critical Essays.* Englewood Cliffs, NJ: Prentice-Hall, 1974. A collection of essays on Baldwin's works.

David Leeming, *James Baldwin: A Biography.* New York: Knopf, 1994. A detailed biography by one of Baldwin's closest friends during the last decade of his life.

C. Eric Lincoln, ed., *Martin Luther King, Jr.: A Profile.* New York: Hill and Wang, 1970. A collection of essays on King.

Margaret Mead and James Baldwin, *A Rap on Race.* Philadelphia: J. B. Lippincott, 1971. A published conversation between Baldwin and anthropologist Margaret Mead.

"The Nation," *Time,* May 17, 1963. An article examining Baldwin's role in the Civil Rights movement.

Horace A. Porter, *Stealing the Fire: The Art and Protest of James Baldwin.* Middletown, CT: Wesleyan University Press, 1989. A study of Baldwin's literary works, focusing on their value as vehicles of social protest.

Orville Prescott, "Books of the Times," *New York Times*, May 19, 1953. A review of *Go Tell It on the Mountain*.

Peter S. Prescott, "The Dilemma of a Native Son," *Newsweek*, December 14, 1987. A tribute that appeared in *Newsweek* shortly after Baldwin's death.

Fred L. Standley and Nancy V. Burt, eds., *Critical Essays on James Baldwin*. Boston: G. K. Hall, 1988. This collection includes reviews and critical essays on Baldwin's works.

James M. Washington, ed., *I Have a Dream: Writings and Speeches That Changed the World*. San Francisco: HarperSan Fran-cisco, 1992. A collection of Martin Luther King Jr.'s most famous speeches.

W. J. Weatherby, *James Baldwin: Artist on Fire*. New York: Donald I. Fine, 1989. A detailed critical biography of Baldwin. Weatherby re-creates Baldwin's life and explores the themes and strategies used in his major works.

Sanford Wexler, *The Civil Rights Movement: An Eyewitness History*. New York: Facts On File, 1993. A pictorial history of the Civil Rights movement that includes time sequences of major events and eyewitness testimonies from the people involved.

Richard Wright, *Native Son*. New York: Harper & Row, 1940. Wright's searing novel had a profound effect on Baldwin as he began his literary career.

Index

Picture Credits

Cover photo: Walter Duran/Archive Photos

AP/Wide World Photos, 42, 47, 49 (bottom), 50, 52 (bottom), 58 (bottom), 59, 62, 66, 67, 72 (top), 75

Archive Photos, 25, 33, 38, 55, 81

Archive Photos/AFP, 16

Gordon Baer/Black Star, 11, 69, 72 (bottom), 73

The Bettmann Archive, 10, 15, 29

Walter Duran/Archive Photos, 27

Henry Hammond/Archive Photos, 13

Matt Herron/Black Star, 57 (bottom)

Bern Keatin/Black Star, 30

Library of Congress, 45, 54 (both), 58 (top)

Reuters/Bettmann, 34, 70

Arnold Sacks/Archive Photos, 56

Steve Schapiro/Black Star, 77, 78

UPI/Bettmann, 14, 20, 37, 43, 44, 48, 49 (top), 52 (top), 57 (top), 65, 76

UPI/Corbis-Bettmann, 9, 39

About the Author

James Tackach teaches American literature at Roger Williams University in Bristol, Rhode Island. His books include *Historic Homes of America*, *Great American Hotels*, and biographies of Henry Aaron and Roy Campanella for young readers. His articles have appeared in the *New York Times*, the *Providence Journal*, and a variety of academic journals. He lives in Narragansett, Rhode Island.